I0605483

Praise for World of Wonders

This beautiful book illuminates what God has in store for us, and in story for us. With Jeff Crosby as our guide, we see how best to number our days along with the pages. The wonder of reading unfurls the glory of God—a God who is lo! with us always—to the very last page.

—**Dr. Carolyn Weber**, author of *Surprised by Oxford* (from the foreword)

World of Wonders is itself a wonder. In this delightful and inspiring book, Jeff Crosby shows us how reading deepens our spiritual lives, even when we may not initially be aware of it doing so. While reading it, I was reminded of so many books and writers who have influenced me over my life. Crosby's clear and wise writing illuminates, as do the vignettes from other authors sprinkled throughout the book. And the reading lists for each section are delightful. As we Quakers say, this book speaks to my condition. I'm sure it will yours as well.

—**J. Brent Bill**, author of *Holy Silence* and *Amity: Stories from the Heartland*

As I read through *World of Wonders*, it created two surprising images for me. First, I felt like I was with Earnest Shackleton sailing the infamous Drake Passage, battling hurricane force winds and waves over a hundred feet high and like him, telling myself, "No doubt Providence guided us." Second, I felt a kinship to John Muir strapped to a California Sierra Douglas Spruce during a violent December storm. Muir said, "Never before did I enjoy so noble an exhilaration of motion." Crosby's book brought me to the Southern Ocean and to the California Sierra. Good books and good reading do that. Crosby's book is rightly named and an adventure worth taking. Read this book. Go exploring.

—**J. K. Jones**, author of *Reading With God in Mind* and *A Soul's House*

World of Wonders is a heartfelt tribute to the transformative power of reading. Crosby's depth and breadth of personal vignettes are deftly woven with profound insights, making a compelling case for reading as a spiritual discipline. From soulful reflections on spiritual growth to prescriptive tools, this book is a treasure trove for anyone seeking to deepen their faith through literature. It's more than just a guide—it's also an invitation to embark on a lifelong journey of wonder, curiosity, and connection. A must-read for avid readers, would-be readers, and spiritual seekers alike.

—**J. Dana Trent**, author *Between Two Trailers*

Most book lovers love that genre of writing—books about books. They are beloved and often influential. *World of Wonders* is one that is unlike any other in this field, a truly lovely, easy-to-read, utterly delightful, deeply spiritual book that indeed makes you want to read more. It helps you realize God's presence as you turn the pages and guides you to encounter the world of wonder that is discovered in an open-hearted reading life. No stuffy tome for only the erudite experts, this is a book for you, me, your neighbors, friends, and even those who may not (yet) love to read. This book is a gift. Read and share.

—**Byron Borger**, Hearts & Minds Books, Dallastown, Pennsylvania

Having been an English teacher and language arts administrator on both high school and college levels during my 40-year career in education, it is easy for me to say that our national education community would greatly benefit from Jeff Crosby's refined celebration about the mesmerizing holiness of reading. I highly recommend *World of Wonders*!

—**Christopher de Vinck**, contributing columnist for *The Dallas Morning News*, author of *Things That Matter Most*

In *World of Wonders*, Crosby has given us a wonderfully written, intimate bit of memoir. Woven throughout are excerpts from great writers, across all genres. With these quotes, we are shown the way in which reading has been formational in this author's journey, and we discover the joy to be found within our own pages.

—**Rick Lewis**, Logos Bookstore, Dallas, Texas

C. S. Lewis wrote, "Heaven, once attained, will work backward." In that sense, Jeff Crosby's book is heavenly, as it works its way backward in your life, revealing that your reading was really a companioning, with the great Companion from whom all creativity comes. After reading *World of Wonders*, I no longer see the books on my shelf as a home library; I see them as a spiritual record of my time here. What a gift.

—**Dr. Kelly Flanagan**, author of *The Unhiding of Elijah Campbell* and *True Companions*

Crosby's book not only traces the way the magic of reading captured his own imagination, setting him on a lifelong career in the book industry. More than that, his exploration of reading as an act of worship, a form of liturgy, and even a spiritual discipline, summons all of us, calling us forth from the frenzy and fragmentation of modern life to the sacred and healing ground of getting lost in a book. It is a stream of shining waters for a fatigued and thirsty soul.

—**Wendy Murray**, journalist and author of *Clare of Assisi, Gentle Warrior* and *The Franciscan Way*

If spiritual disciplines are practices to help us encounter God's grace, then Jeff Crosby is onto something important. What's more, he's the consummate storyteller who brings decades of experience reading, writing, editing, selling, and publishing a variety of books and genres. His wisdom is as evident as his breadth of reading in these pages, gently pointing us toward grace in the various seasons of life.

—**Mark R. McMinn**, co-author of *An Invitation to Slow*

Jeff Crosby appropriately begins his exploration of reading with a quotation from C. S. Lewis's brilliant *Experiment in Criticism,* which, with the perceptive precision typical of Lewis, perfectly describes why we read: "We want to see with other eyes, to imagine with other imaginations, to feel with other hearts, as well as with our own." *World of Wonders* is intended to help us do just that. Despite his immersion in every aspect of book reading and publishing, Jeff is an unintimidating, disarmingly gentle and humble guide for readers of every level of proficiency and every type of reading intention, whether it's for sheer entertainment or deepest spiritual discipline. And don't miss the dozen reading lists, reflecting decades of experience of a veteran reader and publisher. Pure gold.

—**Warren Farha**, founder and owner, Eighth Day Books, Wichita, Kansas

This book invites me to step away from my fragmented life of screens, information, images, and opinion, and returns me to earlier days when I dwelled in books, when I lost track of time, when the now-rare experience of "presence" was as natural as reading. Where researchers fail to spark a change in my habits (despite their evidence of my changing brain and shrinking capacity for attention), *World of Wonders* speaks to my soul through literary quotes, intriguing book lists, practical strategies, and stories of people who call me back to what I once knew—that to read deeply is to inhabit the world more fully and to encounter the God who is there.

—**Karen Wright Marsh**, author of *Wake Up To Wonder* and *Vintage Saints and Sinners*, and executive director of Theological Horizons.

As an avid reader, I saw myself in many of the stories sprinkled throughout *World of Wonders.* As an author, I appreciated Jeff's critical exploration not just of the types of books he most gravitates toward, but also of a myriad of genres, offering compelling, spiritual reasons to explore them. As a pastor, I found myself thinking of particular parishioners that I cannot wait to share this book with. Certainly, it will encourage and challenge those who already love books. But it will also help reluctant readers who are deeply devoted followers of Jesus to find new ways to encounter God. Jeff's stories and real-life examples of meeting God in the pages of books will challenge and encourage others to do the same.

—**Jen Bradbury**, Sr. Director of Family Ministries, First Presbyterian Church, Glen Ellyn, Illinois, and author of *Faith Beyond Youth Group*

WORLD OF WONDERS

A Spirituality of Reading

JEFF CROSBY

Foreword by Carolyn Weber

PARACLETE PRESS
BREWSTER, MASSACHUSETTS

2025 First Printing

World of Wonders: A Spirituality of Reading

ISBN 978-1-64060-945-7

Library of Congress Control Number: 2025016766

10 9 8 7 6 5 4 3 2 1

Published by Paraclete Press
Brewster, Massachusetts
www.paracletepress.com

Printed in United States of America

Dedicated to Cindy

For helping me see the world of wonders
on printed pages—and in the natural world

"When I walk with Jesus, a considerable crowd of unlikely saints walk with me, giving me encouragement for the journey, an invitation to join in a conversation which began long before we were born and shall continue long after we are dead—God, rendered through literature, ancient and modern, God with us as the Word made flesh, then made words so that we might be the Word enfleshed again."

—William H. Willimon
Reading with Deeper Eyes[1]

Contents

FOREWORD

I have been tutored in the spiritual life through the wonder of books.

—Jeff Crosby

My calves burned as my ankles made slow, arduous circles. Gripping the handlebars, I stood almost straight up, pushing the balls of my feet into the worn pedals. August humidity closed in around me, stinging my eyes with sweat I couldn't wipe away. I needed to bear down on the handlebars; this was the steepest part of the hill now. My thighs ached with the effort. My breath came in hard gasps. Just when I thought I couldn't take another breath, I couldn't pump my legs around another wobbling rotation, it appeared: the pointed rooftop of the otherwise flat building, modern (for then) and sleek, set against the rising vista of the city behind it. More and more of the familiar brickwork came into view, until suddenly I crested the hill and plateaued. I collapsed onto the seat, pulled up my sore legs. My bike picked up speed on its own now, hesitantly at first, and then with wild abandonment, until I swept into the pockmarked parking lot—triumphant!—with a wide, swooping arc.

I leaned my sparkle-blue Raleigh against the wall, lodging the basket's rim into the mortar for good measure. I then pulled open the front door with the darkened glass. Stunned blind from having come in directly from the sun, I felt cool air immediately wash over me, prickling the sweat on my skin with a million needles. I closed my eyes, shivering, and breathed in deeply. That scent. *That scent.* The one that remains the same, no matter the geographical or architectural location.

The scent of books. Lots and lots of books!

Cycling to the library during the summers as a child was my favorite pastime. A world of wonders lay only a few blocks away. My bike was a fierce steed, ready for battle. He and I were one, mounting the treacherous hill stretching out mercilessly behind my neighborhood school all the way up, up, up toward the Castle. (Okay, so the castle was really a 1970s municipal building resembling the Brady Bunch house, but oh, my bike was a pretty ride.) I dismounted, part Knight, part Princess, depending on my mood, and entered the dragon's lair, alert for whatever story lured me, also dependent upon my mood. I often judged books by their covers.

But sometimes riding my bike to the library was more than a diversion from summer heat; rather, the journey, as often journeys do, entailed much, much more.

The library served as a haven from the discord of my own family, at times: a physical avoidance from my troubled father's ominous presence, an emotional escape from my mother's heavy sadness. When the dog bites, when the bee stings, when I was feeling sad, I simply remembered the library nearby and then I didn't feel so bad. Charles Van Doren opens his tome from a lifetime of loving books entitled *The Joy of Reading* with the declaration "Reading is my favourite thing to do." Reading was my favorite thing to do, too. And sometimes, it was my only way of surviving—a book can become a floating spar to those who sink and rise and sink and rise and sink again.

Jeff Crosby's book here similarly grows from a lifetime of loving books, loving reading, and loving readers. It is a unique book, in that it is a book about reading, and about what and how to read, and even suggestions for when. It is a book about seasons, of inner as well as outer weather. And it is a book, most of all, about how the wonder of story heals the wounds of our stories. As Harold Bloom puts it in *How to Read and Why*: "Reading well is one of the great pleasures that solitude can afford you, because it is, at least in my experience, the most healing of pleasures."[1]

Thus, this book is written wholeheartedly for anyone in need of enjoyable restoration, which is pretty much everyone I know. It is also for the reader and non-reader alike. If you do not read books, Jeff Crosby offers you an invitation to begin. If you do like to read, he encourages you to read more. And if you already read voraciously, he welcomes you to read intentionally. *World of Wonders: A Spirituality of Reading* is chock full not only of literary ideas, but of practical lists, suggestions, and resources, too.

For any reader on any point in the spectrum, however, Crosby most inspires us to read with discernment. As Leland Ryken explains, "The idea of a 'discerning reader' is not simply that of the ideally responsible reader longed for by authors, but a measure of more than literary competence. In the New Testament, discernment is used in the context of the spiritual, of what is good and bad, and of a process of purity and maturity in seeing what the real purpose of an individual, or a community or even God, might be."[2]

Years after riding my bike to that little local library, I would become a Christian during my graduate studies at Oxford University. The libraries were much larger there, and much older, too. But the scent somehow remained the same; the fragrance of Christ, I now see, wafted through the ages on all those pages, regardless of where one might be.

When I first began reading the Bible, I was not a Christian. By the time I finished it, I was. There arises a power from the Bible that is unique and holy and ultimately, inexplicable. But as a trained reader, as a lover of words, I began to then see how in the unfolding of the Biblical story, every other story, including each of ours, was enfolded within it. In the end, as intimated in the beginning, all would be well. And so I began to see along the way how every story I had ever read, every piece of literature—whether it be a poem, fiction, or nonfiction—points to this Great Story. The questioning trust of the reader eventually leads to reading itself as praise. And the wonder that arises as new worlds open before us as we open each book, stretches out to connect us to the spiritual discipline of learning to love ourselves, others, and our God in ever-deepening ways.

Why read literature, though, especially "stories of what never happened and entering vicariously into feelings which we should try to avoid having in our own person? Or of fixing our inner eye earnestly on things that can never exist? The nearest I have yet got to an answer," writes C. S. Lewis, "is that we seek an enlargement of our being. We want to be more than ourselves. . . . We want to see with other eyes, to imagine with other imaginations, to feel with other hearts, as well as with our own."[3] The spiritual discipline of reading with love brings us continuously closer to God. For, as Lewis concludes, "Good reading, therefore, though it is not essentially an affectional or moral or intellectual activity, has something in common with all three. In love we escape from our self into one another." In the compassionate imagination, we lose ourselves in God and thereby gain our souls.

I have experienced the joy of Jeff Crosby's love and discernment of reading firsthand. As he is a longtime dear family friend as well as a respected publishing colleague, I can attest to his impressive well-read expertise, which he never flounces but humbly keeps quietly pocketed away, only to bring out gently as a well-timed gift. Over the years, Jeff has gifted not only my husband and me with meaningful books that always seemed to come at just the right time, but also our children. They would gather with bated breath at the door whenever he pulled up to visit us in Canada. Despite a busy work schedule, Jeff always made time to drop in and dispense books, like Christmas gifts to wide-eyed Pevensie children—gifts that would become vital at times of need. Which, of course, is what books at their core truly are.

On one visit, in which my husband and I were in need of light and hope and healing, Jeff gifted us with a book aptly entitled *Wonder: Moments that Keep you Falling in Love with Life*. Upon the sudden loss of his dear friend, the author Arthur Gordon writes:

> With life and death placed so abruptly side by side, values shifted, and I seemed to see certain things sharp and plain: that we had been right, not wrong, to risk what we had been risking; that the true measure of life was not the acquisition of money or power or reputation—it was companionship and fulfillment and awareness; that intensity of awareness was the greatest of gifts—and that, therefore, no one should ever feel guilty for seeking out places or experiences where this

> awareness might be found. If anything, the guilt lay in not searching for them more eagerly and more often—for no one has unlimited time.[4]

Yes, so many books and so little time! Always the lament of the bibliophile. But in Christ, we have an eternity of love unimaginable in which to be in the Word, in all its love and everlasting glory. And on this side of heaven, reading provides a glimpse into the adventure before us! For, as it is written:

> What no eye has seen, nor ear heard,
> nor the heart of man imagined,
> what God has prepared for those who love him. (1 Cor. 2:9)

Later still, my hometown library would become my church upon my return from England to Canada. How wondrous that this building of books was transformed into a place of worship! How joyous that one journey would anticipate the other. *World of Wonders* is a book that opens our eyes to such circles of grace. It celebrates the Author of All.

This beautiful book illuminates what God has in store for us, and in story for us. With Jeff Crosby as our guide, we see how best to number our days along with the pages. The wonder of reading unfurls the glory of God—a God who is lo! with us always—to the very last page.

—Dr. Carolyn Weber
Author of *Surprised by Oxford*

"We read books to nourish our capacity to think, to reason, to know, to discern, to remember. The best writing engages the whole of us: heart, mind, body and emotions in an integrated fashion."

—Liz Hoare, from *Twelve Great Spiritual Writers*[1]

Introduction A WORLD OF WONDERS

It was an odd book that, viewed in hindsight, provided the early spark for a life spent in vocational work with words: An unassuming autobiography written by a Russian woman who was on a search for the American father she had never known, published during the latter decades of Cold War tensions between the Soviet Union and the United States.

If memory serves me correctly, I saw the book's author, Victoria Fyodorova, interviewed on the television news program *Good Morning America* in 1979, then hosted by Joan Lunden and David Hartman. Whatever program created my awareness of the book, with certainty I can say that my attention was *immediately* arrested. Something about her life captured my interest, perhaps the vivid details of interesting people and places in her country of origin, which I'd known through US media and public-school textbooks only as a menacing enemy. Or it may have been her search for her American father, whom the book would suggest had never known of his Russian daughter born in 1946. As quickly as I could, I picked up the book at the nearest library some 15 miles from my home and devoured it like a morning bowl of Cap'n Crunch breakfast cereal. It was as if a whole new world—Moscow,

Petrograd, Ukraine, Siberia—was opened to my sheltered North American mind in a profound way, and I sensed for the first time that books were not simply something to be picked up as required by teachers and quickly set aside during the school year, but rather, were portals to a broad world of wonders, people, ideas, places, and stories.

The book was titled *The Admiral's Daughter* and was published in 1979 by a company called Delacorte Press, whose office was at 1 Dag Hammarskjöld Plaza in New York. That address would become significant to me just a few years later when I encountered the book *Markings*, an enduring spiritual classic written by Dag Hammarskjöld, a former secretary-general of the United Nations, published posthumously in 1964. In time, *Markings* would become a touchstone in my reading as a spiritual discipline, returned to again and again for nourishment, insight, reflection, and companionship, especially in seasons of grief and doubt.

But at the time, it was Fyodorova, her search for her father, the setting in an unfamiliar country, and pages of geopolitical intrigue that captured my imagination. Until encountering *The Admiral's Daughter,* my reading life outside of required schoolwork consisted almost entirely of sports pages in daily newspapers, brief biographies of sports legends such as Jackie Robinson, Lou Gehrig, and Henry Aaron, and the Sunday morning *Indianapolis Star*'s comics page featuring *Peanuts*, *Beetle Bailey*, and *Snuffy Smith*.

From that moment in 1979 to the present day, I have metaphorically "traveled" around the world and met thousands of interesting people, encountered remarkably divergent ideas and perspectives, and had windows on the world unlocked and thrown wide open through a life committed to reading as a spiritual discipline.

And I have been tutored in the spiritual life through the wonder of books.

"We want to see with other eyes, to imagine with other imaginations, to feel with other hearts, as well as with our own," C. S. Lewis wrote in the epilogue of his classic work *Experiment in Criticism*. "We are not content to be Leibnitzian monads. We demand windows. Literature as Logos is a series of windows, even of doors. One of the things we feel after reading a great work is 'I have got out'. Or from another point of view, 'I have got in'; pierced the shell of some other monad and discovered what it is like inside."[2]

Oh, the joy of "getting out," and "getting in" through the engagement with literature, old and new.

~

"Has it ever occurred to you that the acts of reading and meditation resemble each other in many ways?" Nancy M. Malone asks in *Walking a Literary Labyrinth: A Spirituality of Reading.* "Both are usually done alone, in silence and physical stillness, our attention focused."[3]

Indeed it has occurred to me. And perhaps it has for you, as well.

Throughout more than 40 years of work in the world of wonders that is the reading, writing, publishing, and selling of books across many Christian traditions, literary genres, and publishing formats, I have come to see the act of reading as a decidedly spiritual discipline, not unlike meditation, prayer, silence and solitude, and fasting. And not just the reading of the Bible—short passages of Scripture quietly, reflectively, and repeatedly in *lectio divina* fashion, which is more commonly understood as a spiritual discipline. Reading across all genres and in all the seasons of our life can prompt growth, change, and connection to God, our neighbors, and to other people. In reading our world is expanded, our minds are challenged, our hearts are attuned to the still small voice of a God who is there and continues to speak through Scripture, yes, but also through the ideas and imaginations and stories of other people who are created in the image of God and who wrestle with many of the same questions we do and who harbor many of the same dreams.

Similarly, reading to children or grandchildren plants seeds of wonder in their rapidly expanding hearts and minds, nurtures their imaginations, and models a life of curiosity that serves them well throughout their lives.

The writer Richard J. Foster first introduced me to the practice of spiritual disciplines when in 1978 he published *Celebration of Discipline: The Path to Spiritual Growth*, a work that has become a beloved classic in the field. He wrote that "the disciplines are God's way of getting us into the ground; they put us where he can work within us and transform us. By themselves, the spiritual disciplines can do nothing; they can only get us to the place where something can be done. They are God's means of grace."[4] Foster's chapter on the discipline of study incorporated thoughts on reading books that will form something of a foundation for what follows, but we will explore genres that go well beyond what he highlighted those many years ago—as he would no doubt wish for us to do.

Some writers wisely suggest caution about labeling as a "spiritual discipline" anything that the Bible does not explicitly give that designation to. Donald S. Whitney, whose book *Spiritual Disciplines for the Christian Life* was formative for me when it was published in the early 1990s and remains so to this day, would be one such person. He suggested that the disciplines he wanted to guide readers into were those "practices found in Scripture that promote spiritual growth among believers in the gospel of Jesus Christ" and which are "habits of devotion and experiential Christianity that have been practiced by the people of God since biblical times."[5]

And yet even Whitney, in a later book titled *Simplify Your Spiritual Life: Spiritual Disciplines for the Overwhelmed,* featured poignant instruction on reading books—even if only one page a day—as a discipline in our Christian journey. In an interview the author and pastor J. K. Jones, another admirer of Whitney's work, asserted that "any practice that causes me to love God more and my neighbor, while bringing me into God's presence where God does the necessary transformative work, is a spiritual discipline." I could not agree more.

What I am suggesting in these pages is to approach our reading life with the same spirit of joy, expectation, and discipline that we do others that Scripture is quite clear about, such as prayer, fasting, solitude, and confession, among others.

Reading as a spiritual discipline requires the same posture that other disciplines ask of us: an open heart, attentiveness, repetition, intentionality, and an invitation to God for God to speak into our life as we practice the discipline—and an expectation that in God's grace and mercy and goodness, God will speak, and our lives will be transformed. It's reading between the lines of the text in what we read, as the late Eugene Peterson suggests in his book *Take and Read*. And importantly, reading as a spiritual discipline is wisely understood, like fasting, meditation, prayer, solitude, and silence, to be life-giving and not yet another "should on ourselves," in the words of the late spirituality writer Brennan Manning.

In this book, you will be met wherever you are on the spectrum of readership—whether prolific or only the occasional as time permits, whether a long-term practitioner or merely an aspiring one—and you'll be invited on a journey to see the ways in which reading deepens, sharpens, and widens our faith, our awareness of the needs around us, and our connection to God. You will glean practical suggestions for finding the world of wonders waiting for you through the practice of reading as a spiritual discipline.

Our journey will take us through a variety of genres including fiction, poetry, and nonfiction. We will consider the reasons that drinking water from not only deep but also diverse wells serves us well in our spiritual journey and our understanding of the experiences and perspectives of others. We'll discover ways to read Scripture as part of this spiritual discipline. And we will look at reading through the seasons of our lives.

Additionally, at the end of each chapter you'll find short vignettes from well-established authors and dedicated readers who illuminate that chapter's content with their own insights. It's my hope that you will find these voices to be additional light upon your path of spiritual reading.

World of Wonders is not an academic book, but reading as a spiritual discipline *does* ask something of us all. It asks for deep, consistent reading, reflecting, and responding. And I believe there is a payoff for us in that.

In an essay titled "Good Reading: Is Digital Culture Reducing Our Ability to Think deeply?," the Wheaton College (Illinois) scholar Mark Talbot suggests that "we can't speed read our way to intellectual, moral, and spiritual depth. The rhythm of deep reading involves looking down at the text to understand and then looking up to reflect. With scripture's aid, this kind of life can help orient (us) regarding some of the moral, political, and spiritual conundrums of our day."[6]

I believe in the power of books to transform lives, to open windows on the world, to fire our imaginations, and to help us be more faithful Christ followers. I believe in the power of books to bridge differences, foster understanding, and offer hope and healing. I have seen it in the lives of others and witnessed it in my own life. But if we are honest, we are increasingly pulled in other directions: technology, work demands, recreational interests, scrolling and swiping on our phones and tablets, and more. According to a Pew Research study released in 2022, 75 percent of the American population had read at least one book the prior year and the average person (the median) had read just four. As a writer and a former publisher, I wish those numbers were higher than they are, and in some countries (France, Spain, Canada, and South Korea), the numbers are, indeed, much higher. But whether you characteristically read one, four, or scores of books annually, there is something for you to ponder in these pages. And, I hope, there are words of encouragement to you, as well.

When it comes to the value of reading books, bestselling essayist Anne Lamott has it right. In her book *Bird by Bird,* Lamott says that "for some of us, books are as important as almost anything else on earth. What a miracle it is that out of these small, flat, rigid squares of paper unfolds world after world after world, worlds that sing to you, comfort you and quiet or excite you. Books help us understand who we are and how we are to behave. They show us what community and friendship mean; they show us how to live and die."[7]

So come along and join me as we look at a world of wonders opened to us through committing to—or continuing—a life of reading as a spiritual discipline. There is much to savor as we walk together with voices from the past, the present, and the future. At the end of each chapter, I offer an annotated list of books that connect to the theme of the content you have just read. Containing voices both contemporary and classic, the books in each chapter's list are among those that have had an imprint on my life as a reader, and perhaps have had (or could have) on yours, as well. Take those lists as a starting (not ending) point as you open a world of wonders through reading as a spiritual discipline.

—Jeff Crosby
September 2024

Part I
Laying the Foundations

"What Camus is saying is that there is reason to be hopeful, that man must understand his condition and must struggle, fight, and rebel against the absurdity of life."

—Jacques Pépin, in his essay on Albert Camus in *The Book That Changed My Life*[1]

Chapter One
WHY READ AT ALL?

I never asked for her name, *and I wish I had.* I never saw her again, *and I'd hoped I would.*

It was a cool autumn Saturday morning in the university community where my wife and I operated a bookstore in the early years of my career working in the world of words. A woman was browsing the store's literature section with her back to me. As I approached to ask her if I could be of help she turned, and I saw two deeply blackened eyes staring back at me. Other seemingly fresh abrasions were clearly visible on both of her cheeks. I also saw tears in her eyes as she asked, "Do you have Albert Camus's *The Stranger* or *The Plague?*"

Although I knew of the French-Algerian novelist and moral philosopher's work from reading his books as an undergraduate just a few years prior to my encounter with this young woman, Camus's works were not among those I devoted shelf space to. After responding with the words no bookseller wants to utter—"No, I'm sorry, we do not but we could order them for you"—I asked the young woman, who I presumed to be an Indiana University student, "Are you okay? You seem to have been hurt."

She deflected my question and instead proceeded to speak with restrained emotion about the absurdity of life, the fallenness and hopelessness of the world—all themes that Camus powerfully addressed in his novels in the 1940s and 50s, including the two she was searching for.

I will never know what had happened to that woman, but I do know that in the midst of whatever trauma and pain she had encountered she made her way to a bookstore seeking in the pages of books what she believed were either answers to, comfort for, or validation of her experience in the world.

And she was not alone then in doing so. Nor are we today when we seek similar outcomes from our reading.

Why We Read

In his book *How to Read and Why,* Yale University humanities professor Harold Bloom offers a candid and sober answer to his question (and ours in this chapter).

> "You can read merely to pass the time, or you can read with an overt urgency, but eventually you will read against the clock. Bible readers, those who search the Bible for themselves, perhaps exemplify the urgency more plainly than readers of Shakespeare, yet the quest is the same," Bloom states. "One of the uses of reading is to prepare ourselves for change, and the final change alas is universal."[2]

All of us read for many different reasons in different seasons of our lives. Sometimes we are searching for escape. At other times we are looking for answers to a vexing question or to find consolation in the midst of crushing grief. Some days we are looking for help in raising a child or, later in life, caring for aging parents whose health is rapidly declining and presenting to our families profound issues we had hoped to avoid—or didn't think about at all until forced to do so. We read the Bible as a means of understanding the way of Jesus, or in the hope of finding guardrails to avoid in our home the type of chaotic life we grew up with in our families of origin or, conversely, to understand what made our families "work" so we can replicate that. We read to solve problems, or to persuade other people of our point of view or, on our good days, to understand the way other people see the world. We read to our children and grandchildren and, if we are lucky, they will read to us one day if we can no longer manage the task ourselves. We read to be what the journalist David Brooks in his book *How to Know a Person* calls a "good conversationalist." That is, to be someone who "is a master of fostering a two-way exchange."[3]

"Books draw us deeply into the lives of others, showing us the world through someone else's eyes, page after page," Anne Bogel writes in *I'd Rather Be Reading.* "They take us to new and exciting places while meeting us right where we are, whisking us away to walk by the Seine or through a Saharan desert or down a Manhattan sidewalk. Books provide a safe space to encounter new and unfamiliar situations, to practice living in unfamiliar environments, to test-drive encounters with new people and new experiences."[4]

In the 1993 film *Shadowlands,* an adaptation of a script originally written as a play that focused on the relationship of C. S. Lewis and Joy Davidman, the actor Anthony Hopkins (as the Oxford professor Lewis) greets his new student, Chadwick, in his tutoring room. As he first lights and then quickly begins to puff on his pipe, he makes a statement.

"We read to know we are not alone," the Lewis character says. And then he poses a question to the young Chadwick: "Do you think that's so?"

Chadwick replies, "Well, I hadn't thought about it like that before, sir." After a brief pause, Lewis succinctly responds, "No, nor did I."

It's a lovely and memorable encounter in the film containing words—"we read to know we're not alone"—that are now affixed to greeting cards, printed on posters, and emblazoned on coffee mugs with Lewis's name attached despite the fact there is no evidence that Lewis ever made that *precise* statement in his books or lectures.

Nonetheless, I have come to believe that what the actor Hopkins said in his role as Lewis is true. Reading helps us have a sense of belonging, understanding, companionship. A sense of being known. That has certainly been true for me. Some of the richest conversations I have throughout each year, whether with my wife, a close friend, or a new business partner, are built around the question, "Tell me what you're reading that you're highly recommending and why?" and the common response of reciprocity, "And what about you?"

We also read, I believe, to know that God is there, is not silent, is speaking to us through the *logos*, the Word—and through words. This is not something peculiar to the West, or to my own context. It is, I believe, something like a universal reality.

Reading Around the World

I recently attended an exhibit of more than 100 profoundly moving images taken by the famed photographer Steve McCurry. He may be best known for his 1984 portraiture of the green-eyed Afghan girl Sharbat Gula in a refugee camp outside Peshawar, Pakistan, in the midst of the Soviet Union's invasion of her home country. That image was among those gathered at the Loyola University Museum of Art in Chicago for the ICONS exhibit. As I suspected, it was riveting to come face-to-face with the image of Gula and her piercing green eyes in the photo that initially graced the June 1985 cover of *National Geographic* accompanying a story titled "Along Afghanistan's War-Torn Frontier." Other images of people and places from around the world—Syria, India, Madagascar, Bangladesh, Nepal, Myanmar—and closer to home, including the September 11, 2001, devastation around New York City's World Trade Center towers, graced the walls of several galleries in the museum. The images told stories of war, resilience, suffering, hope, family and cultures. But there was another aspect of ICONS that I didn't expect to see.

A homage to the beauty, allure, and practice of reading around the world.

In room after room of the gallery, McCurry's photos captured images of people reading in the midst of rubble and work and want and play. Sacred texts of the religions of the world spread out before readers on the ground, eyes attentively fixed on the pages. Newspapers being read on the trunk of a taxicab in Mumbai, or on the platform of a train station in Kolkata. One of the most striking images showed a young man sitting on a large stone reading a paperback book, his back propped up against a massive elephant curled around the stone like a pillow.

What was it about reading around the world that captured the eyes and trained the lens of the famed photographer Steve McCurry?

"Reading is a serious matter, but readers are seldom lonely or bored, because reading is a refuge and an enlightenment," writes Paul Theroux in the foreword to a collection of McCurry's images in the book *Steve McCurry: On Reading*. "This wisdom is sometimes visible. It seems to me that there is always something luminous in the face of a person in the act of reading."[5]

The Singer, His Song and Impact

I have no idea whether or not there was luminosity on my face on the day I first encountered the Christian book that set me on the course of working in writing, bookselling, and publishing. But I can imagine there was.

More than 40 summers ago when I joined my soon-to-be-wife, Cindy, for her family's vacation in the north woods of Wisconsin, I took along a slim, oddly shaped book she or perhaps her mother had given me, titled *The Singer*. It was written by Calvin Miller, a man I'd never heard of, and it had mesmerizing sketches scattered through its pages, which added a mysterious, evocative texture to the poetic prose. Together the words and images drew me in, captivating my attention to an unusual degree.

As the aging blue Chevy van rumbled its way north for hours on end through the Midwestern farmlands of the United States, I read

Miller's retelling of the Christ of the Gospel of Matthew, written in the narrative tradition of J. R. R. Tolkien and C. S. Lewis, two writers I *had* heard of but whose works I had not yet read. That would come later, influenced no doubt by the impact and enjoyment of *The Singer* and its sequels, *The Song* and *the Finale.*

When I opened the cover of *The Singer* on that summer morning as our journey began, I found the opening words were situated not in the customary location but rather on the bottom left-hand side of the page, with type set in a manner not like a work of prose but rather like poetry:

> For most who live,
> hell is never knowing
> who they are.
> The Singer knew and
> knowing was his torment.

Calvin Miller had me hooked from line one of *The Singer.*

My reading tastes in that summer of 1982 were decidedly tilted toward twentieth-century history and biography, spurred on by the encounter a few years prior with *The Admiral's Daughter*. Literature of the imaginative and the biblical varieties was not yet on my radar to a significant degree.

The Singer changed that. It also changed my life. It cultivated in me a passion for books, for reading, and for sharing with others the delight of knowing and being known through the power of words. It also served as an inspiration to attempt to write myself.

Years later, Calvin Miller would serve on a panel I moderated at a bookselling event in New York City on "The Power of Story," and a friendship was born. The final time I saw him was in February of 2009 at a café in Dallas, Texas. I had invited him to come for a book industry conference to promote an anniversary edition of *The Singer.* We talked about our respective lives and hopes, our families of origin and our relationships with our fathers, which contained (as most do) a mixture of sadness and joy. But most of our talk centered on the surprising impact of the book he authored—the impact on him, on me, on readers worldwide. I could sense in his voice and his countenance the deep gratitude he carried in his heart.

The musician and author Michael Card spoke for many readers of *The Singer* when for its 25th anniversary edition he wrote, "*The Singer* was not simply a book for me. It was an event. It was the first demonstration in our time that the gospel could be newly presented to the world at the level of the imagination."[6]

Reading in Our Modern Day

What is *your* story? What book has had that kind of impact on your life? As you reflect on your engagement with ideas and people and wonders through the written word, what stands out to you? Has your practice of reading grown or shrunk over time? Or does it simply ebb and flow like the tides? Has it changed in the digital world we all now live in?

Sven Birkerts writes in his influential book *The Gutenberg Elegies: The Fate of Reading in an Electronic Age*, "Fewer and fewer people, it seems, have the leisure or the inclination to undertake (serious reading). And true reading is hard. Unless we are practiced, we do not just crack the covers and slip into an alternate world. We do not get swept up as readily as we might be by the big-screen excitements of film. But if we do read perseveringly we make available to ourselves, in a most portable form, an ulterior existence. We hold in our hands a way to cut against the momentum of the times."[7]

Birkerts's assertion is true for our reading life as a whole, including reading sacred texts and contemporary books that offer a light on our path as we pursue a life of faith. But the reading of books is not the primary point. Even some of the most notorious tyrants of modern history were said to have been voracious readers. It is a *changed* life that is the point. It is the outflow of wisdom, kindness, beauty, truth, goodness, compassion, and patience that is the point. The late Eugene Peterson would call this *spiritual reading.*

"Reading is an immense gift, but only if the words are assimilated, taken into the soul—eaten, chewed, gnawed, received in unhurried delight," Peterson writes. "Words of men and women long dead, or separated by miles and/or years, come off the page and enter our lives freshly and precisely, conveying truth and beauty and goodness, words that God's Spirit has used and uses to breathe life into our souls."[8]

Wherever you are on the spectrum of readers, from those of us who carry multiple books with us at all times in our travel bags to others of us who pick up one only occasionally, recognize the act of reading for what it is: an immense gift, one to which we can devote some measure of time, attentiveness, curiosity, and wonder. May the pages to come deepen your commitment, and may they lead you down rabbit trails of new books, authors, and subjects for your future reading.

On Reading as a Spiritual Discipline

> Reading is such a spiritual discipline for me that I find it difficult to speak on behalf of others regarding the why and how. The why for me in reading is centered on the selflessness of the act. I admit I read to grow in my field of study, to deepen my life's roots, to know that I am not alone, but I fundamentally read to get outside of myself. Reading un-self's me. It is a James 1:19 exercise: "Quick to hear, slow to speak . . ." As for the question of how, I simply give reading priority in my life. I read in small patches of time, ten or 15 minutes here and there, but I also read in large plots of time, a half day here, a whole day there.[9]
>
> **J. K. Jones,** author of *Reading With God in Mind* and *A Soul's House: A Primer for Spiritual Formation*

Why Read At All?

12 Recommended Books on the Reading Life

Below is a list of twelve books that offer insight, inspiration, and practical guidance on the importance and practice of reading. Even if you are already a committed reader, you'll find much to savor. And if you are at the beginning of this journey with the world of wonder found in books, you'll find delightful traveling companions.

- *Reading for the Love of God*, by Jessica Hooten Wilson
- *Reading with God in Mind*, by J. K. Jones
- *Why We Read*, by Shannon Reed
- *Walking a Literary Labyrinth*, by Nancy M. Malone
- *A Book Lover's Guide to Great Reading*, by Terry Glaspey
- *The Gutenberg Elegies*, by Sven Birkerts
- *Reading for the Common Good*, by C. Christopher Smith
- *On Reading Well*, by Karen Swallow Prior
- *Reading with Deeper Eyes*, by William H. Willimon
- *12 Great Spiritual Writers*, by Liz Hoare
- *The Reading Life: The Joy of Seeing New Worlds Through Others' Eyes*, by C. S. Lewis
- *Reality and the Vision*, edited by Philip Yancey

"Books transform our lives and the lives of our friends and neighbors. There's a reason Jesus is called the Word. He was made flesh and dwelt among us. God has given us words from the beginning—words that inspire, inform, and instruct us."

—Byron Borger, *A Book for Hearts & Minds*[1]

Chapter Two
Reading as a Spiritual Discipline: Stories, Practices, Pathways

In the circles I have traveled throughout my career in the world of bookselling, publishing, and writing about matters of faith and practice, the idea of *integration* has increasingly been a guiding light.

I encountered a series of books released under the title "Through the Eyes of Faith" in the 1980s just as I was beginning to explore Christian teachings more deeply and make them my own rather than simply inherited from those around me. Through the reading of those books on a diverse set of subjects including biology, mathematics, literature, history, and psychology I expanded my view of what could be viewed through the lens of faith, theology, Scripture, and logic. The idea that the Christian faith could be integrated with—not bifurcated from—these disciplines (and many others) was both instructive and compelling. What was likely obvious to others had not been.

And now it was.

Booksellers Byron Borger and Beth Borger are people whose work for several decades has exemplified this idea of integration. When you walk into Hearts & Minds Books on the main highway that threads east and west through Dallastown in south central Pennsylvania, you encounter a beautifully curated collection that serves as something of an object lesson for the idea of the integration of faith in all dimensions of study, all aspects of society, all realms of discourse. Whether politics or philosophy, environment or education, literature or linguistics, social justice or salvation, race or religions of the world, the arts or architecture, Hearts & Minds not only exposes its customers to a breadth of books but also engages with each customer on a level that ensures the right work is placed in their hands, their hearts, and their minds at the right time. Why such a commitment?

Worship.

That commitment grows out of the Borgers' understanding of the connection—the integration—between reading and the worship of the living God. It grows out of a desire to see lives transformed via a Christ *in* culture rather than a Christ *against* culture mindset.

Reading as a Part of Our Worship

"I believe reading is *worship*," Byron Borger boldly writes in an essay on reading. "God tells us that we are called to love Him with all our minds. So the mandate to use our minds is not just for intellectuals or scholarly types or philosophers, it's a mandate to all of us to use the gray matter God has given us to think well and read well to His glory. It's an act of worship and an act of love. Reading is a way to love God with our minds and therefore reading can become an act of worship."[2]

As we talk about a spirituality of reading, this foundational idea about the relationship between worship and reading will serve us well. In the New Testament Gospel we read, "And you shall love the Lord your God with all your heart and with all your soul and with all your mind and with all your strength" (Mark 12:30).[3] In Luke's Gospel (10:27), we read a similar message when Jesus says, "You shall love the Lord your God with all your heart and with all your soul and with all your strength and with all your mind, and your neighbor as yourself."[4] The cultivation of the life of the mind, the affections of the heart, and a corresponding love of God and of our neighbor as ourself is not done only through reading, of course. There are many other avenues that are a part of such cultivation, including service, giving, prayer, and the pursuit of justice where injustice is present. But for centuries, reading has been a key aspect of the cultivation of these virtues.

In a book published in association with the spiritual formation ministry Renovaré, founded by Richard J. Foster in 1988, we encounter this idea clearly:

> Throughout the history of the Christian faith Christians have been transformed by spiritual reading. Our primary resource is the Bible, but our life of faith has also been shaped by the writings of many Christians who were seeking to interpret the Bible, further their understanding, and live the Christian life. The goal of spiritual reading is for it to affect who we are and what we do, to transform us.[5]

This resource then goes on to suggest 25 essential readings for us all, from the Russian novelist Dostoyevsky's *The Brothers Karamazov* to the French mathematician and physicist Blaise Pascal's *Pensées*; from G. K. Chesterton's *Orthodoxy* to Thomas Merton's *The Seven Storey Mountain*; from the poetry of Gerard Manley Hopkins to St. Augustine's *Confessions.* In the reading of these classic books, we are encouraged to do so not for *information* but rather for *formation.*

As we seek to cultivate the spiritual discipline of reading we do well to begin with the Bible, whether we read it merely as literature or as the living word of the God in whose image we are made. Christians believe that Scripture has something very special to say to us as it portrays the arc of creation, fall, and redemption and the coming of Christ as Immanuel, "God with us," and the ultimate reality in which all is made new. We are wise to apply the practice of intentional spiritual reading of both the Bible and books throughout the seasons of our life.

The way my friend Hattie Driscoll did.

An Early and a Current Example

When I was in my late 20s and early 30s, each month my wife and I along with our two young children led a worship service at a nursing home/assisted living facility near our home and church. The residents, many of them in wheelchairs, gathered around the piano or near the front where we would play familiar hymns on guitar prior to delivering the brief (and likely largely forgettable) devotional message I would offer. As we sang words that were clearly written on their hearts, the countenance on the residents' faces lifted and they sang with joy. Hattie Driscoll was always there, with a paperback book in one hand and her Bible in the other. Her face was joyful as she sang the hymns that she had likely sung in church services throughout her life.

A woman in her late 80s when we began leading these services, Hattie had bluish-gray hair and an ever-present button-down sweater that evoked images of a female Mr. Rogers. She modeled the notion of reading as a spiritual practice, a Christian commitment. She knew that Cindy and I were booksellers, and invariably she brought to the service a book she had read and felt that I, in turn, simply had to read as well. Long before the advent of online stores, she ordered her books through the Billy Graham Evangelistic Association in Minneapolis and other mail order catalogs. After the service, she would invite me back to her living quarters to tell me about all the books she'd read in the prior month and what she had learned. She would then give me her copy of the book she'd brought to the service, and ask me to bring it back at my next visit and tell her what I thought.

Although I was still young by the time I met Hattie Driscoll, I had for several years been committed to reading as part of my growth in the Christian faith. However, the years of overlap with her gave me a vision for what it looked like to sustain that commitment throughout a life. I remember thinking to myself, "I hope I am still reading with such discipline and passion when I am her age!"

I've never forgotten her example.

Oklahoma native Craig Stoll, who like me has worked in the world of books all of his adult life, is another example of a life devoted to reading as an expression of his faith, his worship of God, and his curiosity about the world we inhabit. Though he had been a reader early in his youth (primarily of books many of us read as part of our elementary education such as E. B. White's *Charlotte's Web*), his lifelong discipline of reading was catalyzed and broadened by his encounter with the canon of Sir Arthur Conan Doyle's *Sherlock Holmes* mysteries.

At the time he read them, Stoll's school and the place of his mother's employment were about eight miles from where his family lived. After school, he would walk two blocks every day to the public library where he would wait for an hour or two for his mother's workday to end. Stoll had come to faith in Christ around this time, and he began to read more out of a desire to deepen his faith and out of curiosity about those volumes he saw each day in that public library.

"I remember that I was looking around the library one afternoon after school and noticed a two-volume set of the entire Holmes collection (four novels and 56 short stories). I don't know why, but I was struck by the thought that it would be an accomplishment to read the whole thing, so made up my mind to try to do that," Stoll told me. "I was hooked and couldn't get enough—something completely new just clicked upon reading the whole canon at that particular time. I do think books affect us in different ways at different times. Whatever happened at that time with Holmes, Watson, and me, I just knew I had found something that delighted me and that would become a lifelong interest."

Stoll continues to re-read the entire original Holmes canon every two to three years, and in the intervening years he will generally read related books, either Doyle's nonfiction or Holmes mysteries by other authors. But his reading has broadened considerably since those days, and it has also impacted his life and the direction of his work in profound spiritual ways.

"I suppose I must have thought that if the Holmes books could be that enjoyable then there must be other books equally as interesting," Stoll said. "At that time I still watched a fair amount of television, but it just seemed reading those books was of a different and higher order that television couldn't match."

Stoll counts books such as A. W. Tozer's *The Knowledge of the Holy*, Dane Ortlund's *Gentle and Lowly*, and Sam Storms's *Convergence* as life-changing books. But it was a memoir with no distinctly Christian message that re-directed Stoll's vocational work in a profound way.

After years of work as a bookseller, Stoll read John Wood's memoir *Leaving Microsoft to Change the World*, and his life's purpose came into focus: the formation of a not-for-profit organization called Christianbook International Outreach, which provides books for international Christian leaders and theological schools without access to them.

"Wood's book came to me at just the right moment and changed my life as God was leading me into the work I now do," Stoll told me. Christianbook International Outreach has now distributed more than two million books and Bibles to pastors, theological students, and churches in more than 80 countries.

In the winter of 2023 as part of his work with the organization he founded, Stoll traveled more than 7,000 miles from his home in New England to Limuru, Kenya, where he delivered a message he titled "Books: God's Tools of Mercy and Transformation." Speaking to a group of students and pastors, Stoll suggested that there are three core ways God uses books to accomplish the objectives of mercy to us and transformation in us:

1. God uses books to help us renew our minds.
2. God uses books to help us better understand and interpret the Bible.
3. God uses books as tools and preparation for ministry.

As he concluded his message that day in Kenya, Stoll exhorted the group of students and pastors to "Read—for the good of your own souls, for the good of the souls of those whom you lead or will someday lead, for the good of your churches and communities, for the good of Kenya and the Kingdom of God!"[6]

It's a message all of us can benefit from paying attention to in our own contexts. How do we cultivate this? What are some practical pathways?

Developing a Liturgy of Reading

We are all shaped by *something*—by our "liturgy" of life—whether or not we recognize it as such. Developing a liturgy of reading, including Scripture and books beyond that for all seasons of our lives, can be nurtured in a variety of ways.

Practices and pathways to becoming (or continuing to be) a disciplined, reflective reader amid all of the distractions and pressures and reasons to not be one include these:

- **Making a commitment of time to read**. I am fortunate in that I am married to a person who reads even more than I do, so our shared passion for reading makes allocating time a "family" activity. For some that may not be the case. Regardless, reading as a spiritual discipline requires time and practice, just as with any other endeavor. Like Shannon Reed, the author of *Why We Read: On Bookworms, Libraries, and Just One More Page Before Lights Out*, I never travel anywhere without a book—one never knows when time may present itself! However, I know that my best reading is done at the beginning and end of each day, when my attention is fixed on what is before me. If I go for any length of time without a clear sense that I have space for reflective spiritual reading, it's a red flag that I am simply too busy (or too distracted) and need to attend to that larger question.

- **Find the format that best fits your patterns of reading**. There's a coffee mug in our family's cabinet that is emblazoned with an antique-looking print book and the words "The Book Was Better" and a bold exclamation mark to end the sentence. People who work in the world of books have strong feelings about publishing formats and preferences. Though I am (and likely will continue to be, provided my eyesight is maintained) a reader primarily of print books, I increasingly find myself format-agnostic. What's important for you as a reader is to find the format that best fits your needs, your lifestyle. What will help you read more, and do so more reflectively? Choose that format, whether audiobook (where production values are now exceedingly high) or digital device such as a Kindle e-reader, where light and type size can be adjusted for people with visual challenges. Companies like Lutheran Braille Workers are making Christian books and Bibles available for the vision impaired.

- **Finding a space (or spaces) that are conductive to reflective reading**. When I traveled to an office each day (which I no longer do), I had a practice of having breakfast or tea at a café on the way, and I would take my reading and a journal with me for reflective reading and response. Today, working and reading in my home in a space with no television but instrumental music playing in the background has been conducive to this activity. For some, listening to audiobooks on their longer commutes is the space most helpful. If you are just experimenting with attempting to read more often and more deeply, try several different spaces and see what works best for you. And then, like the basketball player shooting free throws over and over again to perfect her touch, do it again . . . and again!

- **Have a journal nearby**. I once worked with a colleague who read voraciously, and as he did he took copious notes for virtually all of his spiritual reading. He transferred his handwritten pages into a typed version and catalogued them in binders. His ability to recall teachings and insights he wanted to remember was astounding, and it inspired me to keep a journal nearby as I read. My system is not nearly as refined as my former colleague's, but the very act of journaling in response to important words in my reading has an effect on retention and application.

- **Build lists of books to read**. Curiosity is a wonderful catalyst for becoming a disciplined and reflective reader. Ask others what they are reading and build a list of works that strike a chord of curiosity with you. Share with others what *you* are reading and engender conversations about what you (and they) are learning. Subscribe to blogs such as the one curated by Bob Trube (BobonBooks.com), one of the most diverse sources for book recommendations I have encountered, or read the Englewood Review of Books (EnglewoodReview.org), with its emphasis on community, mission, imagination, and reconciliation. Subscribe to the Hearts & Minds Books newsletter or podcast, available on Spotify, to receive content about books that Byron and Beth Borger are recommending and why.

- **Read and then dialogue in community with others.** While the act of reading is typically done in isolation, quietly and in something of an "internal" dialogue with ourselves and the characters in the novel we are reading or the content of the poetry or nonfiction we hold in our hands, discussing books in community with others can be an opening for a deeper understanding.

- **Intentionally choose to read authors whose perspective is quite distinct from your own.** Classic voices such as Howard Thurman's *Jesus and the Disinherited* or James H. Cone's more recent *The Cross and the Lynching Tree* or the late John Lewis's memoir *Walking with the Wind* illuminated the history and perspectives of African American sisters and brothers. Marlena Graves's *The Way Up is Down* offered a Latina woman's powerful insights on the idea of *memento mori,* or the importance of remembering our own death in order to help us prioritize what is important. Works by the martyred El Salvador priest Oscar Romero such as *The Violence of Love* expanded my view of the church in Latin America. Such choices in our reading take intentionality and an openness to learn from voices that may not be familiar, and which may make us uncomfortable.
- **Share about what you have read and why it's impacted you.** There are many things about our hyper-connected digital world that could be critiqued. But one positive is our ability to write about what we have read and to post insights we have gleaned or about why a book has been important to us. Pull from your journaled notes and post succinct reviews to social media spaces so others can benefit from what you have experienced.

These are eight of the practices I have undertaken and pathways I have traveled in my reading life. Yours may be different. Whatever your practices and pathways are, may we all be like Hattie Driscoll and read (and pass along books!) to the end of our days. May we all be like Byron Borger and see our act of reading as an act of worship. And may we all be like Craig Stoll, recognizing how God is using books for good in our own lives.

And may we give thanks to God for it all.

On Reading as a Spiritual Discipline

When I have been asked "who are your mentors?" I usually refer to authors—even those who are dead! In doing so, I'm not ignoring the great influences pastors, colleagues and others have had on me. But being able to read and reread well-crafted and meaningful experiences of authors' walk with God is a rich source of spiritual understanding and companionship. The first time I read Henri Nouwen's book *In the Name of Jesus,* I felt like he was speaking directly for me and to me. I often feel that way in reading Eugene Peterson or other spiritual writers. So, in my devotions, I almost always read a chapter of a spiritually thoughtful book after I read and reflect on a Scripture passage. Reading both the Word of God and the writings of a person of God helps me to better discern the work of God not only in their lives but also in mine.

Bob Fryling, author of *The Leadership Ellipse: Shaping How We Lead by Who We Are*

Reading, Journaling, and Spiritual Disciplines

12 Recommended Books

Below is a list of twelve books that offer windows into the spiritual disciplines broadly, and journaling specifically, as well as other works on reading that help us make space for the world of wonders found in them.

- *25 Books Every Christian Should Read*, selected by Renovaré and edited by Julia Roller
- *Devotional Classics*, edited by Richard J. Foster and James Bryan Smith
- *Spiritual Classics*, edited by Richard J. Foster and Emilie Griffin
- *Journal Keeping*, by Luann Budd
- *Journaling as a Spiritual Practice*, by Helen Cepero
- *An Unhurried Life*, by Alan Fadling
- *A Book for Hearts & Minds: What You Should Read and Why*, with various contributors including Steven Garber, Byron Borger, David Gushee, and Karen Swallow Prior
- *Books: God's Tools in the History of Salvation*, by Klaus Bockmuehl
- *The Pleasures of Reading in an Age of Distraction*, by Alan Jacobs
- *How to Read and Why*, by Harold Bloom
- *Reading with God in Mind*, by J. K. Jones
- *Deep Reading*, by Rachel B. Griffis, Julie Ooms, and Rachel M. De Smith Roberts

"And yet just because it is a book about both the sublime and the unspeakable, it is a book also about life the way it really is. It is a book about people who at one and the same time can be both believing and unbelieving, innocent and guilty, crusaders and crooks, full of hope and full of despair. In other words it is a book about us."

—Frederick Buechner, *Wishful Thinking*[1]

Chapter Three
Reading Scripture as a Spiritual Discipline: Stories, Practices, Pathways

For a child growing up in the 1960s, expressions of civil religion in America were common occurrences in schools and civic life. Prayers were routinely offered before kickoffs at Friday night high school football games and prior to the running of the annual Indianapolis 500, the "greatest spectacle in racing," as we Hoosiers proudly understood it at the time. Religion also made appearances through prayers and readings before, during, and after legislative sessions at the Indiana Statehouse.

Public encounters with Bible passages were, likewise, common then compared to now. The masthead of the Indianapolis newspaper that my family read daily quoted the New Testament in every issue as it proclaimed, "where the Spirit of the Lord is, there is liberty" (2 Corinthians 3:17). I must have encountered that passage thousands of times before I ever considered what it meant or why the Pulliam family, owners of the newspaper, would have put it there year after year.

Retail stores were largely closed on Sundays in recognition of the privileged place the Christian religious tradition held in the United States (versus Jewish or other faith traditions), and alcohol was not readily available to purchase anywhere on that day. The reading of a Bible text prior to local governmental meetings and social clubs was as common as basketball hoops on the sides of barns that dotted the Indiana landscape.

But even with all of those markers of civil religion, I knew very little about the Bible. My mother had been impacted by a United Methodist Church her grandmother Molly Butler introduced her to as a girl, and she carried that tradition forward by taking my brothers and me to a church in that denomination for a season. I'm sure I heard stories and lessons from the Bible on those occasions, though I have few memories of it.

The Bible was for me the tiny brown or green imitation leather New Testaments that members of the Gideons International would pass out each year to the students in my public elementary school in a small town in west central Indiana. I distinctly recall receiving them and taking them home, but I don't have a memory of ever reading one.

I didn't know the Bible, didn't read it, didn't miss it. And I didn't know I should.

My first memory of being mildly interested in the Bible was on an Easter Sunday sometime in the late 1960s in conjunction with my family's visit to a church. My brothers and I were given a King James "authorized edition" to share among the three of us. Unlike the Gideons' plain, pocket-sized portion, this one was larger and had *both* testaments. More importantly to a young boy used to reading colorful comic strips in the Sunday newspaper, this Bible had vibrant illustrations of Noah and the ark, Moses and the tablets with the Ten Commandments, David and his slingshot felling the giant Goliath, and the parting of something called the Red Sea. It was the first time I took notice of this book that didn't really look or seem like a *normal* book. (What *were* those numbers scattered through the pages all about? Did that flood *really* happen like that? Cool!) Seeds of interest were planted (mostly, looking at those colorful pages, I suspect), and eventually fruit would grow out of that, many years later.

Recognizing the Importance (and Challenge) of Scripture

While attending a church camp in the mid-1970s under the influence of an elderly woman in the small town I grew up in, I was given a *Living New Testament*, a paraphrase that Tyndale House Publishers founder Kenneth N. Taylor worked on for his own children during his commutes on a train from Chicago's western suburbs into the city where he worked at a publishing house. What was good for Taylor's children seemed to be good for me—the common language of his paraphrase of Scripture connected with my own life. The words sounded like those spoken around me, almost like everyday conversation. The vocabulary was easier to digest. Taylor's rendering of Scripture prompted me to begin to read more regularly what had always seemed like an obscure, distant book. Eventually, as an undergraduate student I found my way into a church and began to uncover a sense of why Scripture was so vital in laying the foundations of faith.

Even so, throughout my years as a follower of Christ, my practice of reading Scripture has been marked by ebbs and flows, by seasons of flourishing and others of drought. (I marvel when I meet someone for whom this does not appear to be the case.)

Sometimes this text that is sacred to Christians seems to be chock full of life, wonder, inspiration, and clarity, while at other times it seems obscure, distant, and filled with difficult and tangled-up passages that confound me. After nearly fifty years of reading Scripture, I still have seasons in which it's hard to consistently give it the focus I intellectually believe it deserves.

Is Our Bible Reading Set Up for Failure?

In his remarkable book *The Bible Reset: Simple Breakthroughs to Make Scripture Come Alive*, Alex Goodwin, cofounder of the Institute for Bible Reading (IBR), comes alongside those of us who have struggled with consistent, disciplined reading and application of Scripture and offers us not only an empathetic voice but also practices to consider. His book has become among the most helpful of all Bible reading resources I have encountered.

"From the moment you open the Bible, the odds are stacked against you. The struggle begins with the formatting, which can resemble an overcrowded textbook more than anything else," Goodwin writes with understanding. "On every page, you're confronted by stark pillars of text, often surrounded by a scaffolding of even more text: cross-references, notes, callout boxes, and more."[2]

Beyond the formatting (chapters and verses were added in the thirteenth century by the Archbishop of Canterbury, Stephan Langton[3]), Goodwin suggests that we readers are often not instructed in just what we should do as we read the text. "For some reason, it's just assumed that if we open this book and spend enough time in it, the magic will happen. Like Chia Pet instructions to 'just add water,' we're taught to 'just add Bible' and our faith will grow. We'll come to know God through this book if we just try hard enough."[4]

Does that challenge sound familiar to you? If so, know that you are not alone.

In our reading as a spiritual discipline, it's important to ensure that the Bible is a key part of the time, attention, and focus we commit to. If we attend church services either in person or online, we will (or should) encounter a depth of engagement with the Bible and be guided in making applications to our own lives. Perhaps adult education in the local church is another avenue for engagement with Scripture, while others of us may attend small groups that make Scripture study one of if not the central focus of time together. I have found that the richest explorations in Scripture, however, have come about when I've both immersed myself in the narratives of the Bible text on my own, pondered them in community with others, and listened to Scripture through a variety of mediums and in an assortment of translations. It has been in seasons when those spiritual practices were undertaken that the results have arguably been most transformative. But I have also found that different seasons of life have called for a change in approach to my Bible reading, and it has been important for me to maintain an openness to trying new pathways.

For some of us who are committed to a life of reading, one obstacle to engaging Scripture may be surprising, as it was for a bibliophile in the state of Texas.

Books as a Barrier to Bible Reading

Rick Lewis is a bookseller in Dallas, and like Byron Borger at Hearts & Minds Books in Pennsylvania, he has committed most of his adult life to reading as a spiritual discipline and to recommending books to others. In a recent conversation, he confessed that at times his expansive reading has competed with a disciplined engagement with the Bible.

"During a discussion with my spiritual director about the discipline of fasting, I said (fasting from) food is hard to do because I need regular meals to take the medications I require for my medical condition," he told me. Lewis said the spiritual director responded by saying, "Let's pray and see what God may have to say about fasting for you." He continued, "While praying, she got this big smile and asked if I had ever thought of fasting from reading. My first thought was, I can't do that! My second thought was, I guess I better do that, if I'm that obsessed with my books. So, I fasted from reading anything but Scripture for a month."

Lewis said his fasting from books for that month did two things for him. First, he was able to reconnect with Scripture in new ways because he had more time do dwell in the text and to read it reflectively, slowly, carefully. And second, he started giving himself permission to not finish a book if it wasn't speaking to him—something he had previously simply been unable to do.

I suspect that Lewis and I aren't the only two committed readers who sometimes find our Bible reading taking a back seat to works of theology, spiritual formation, biographies, novels, history, and other genres of writing and publishing. If that strikes you as familiar, you might consider (as I have) setting aside a portion of your reading time specifically to engage with the Bible, either on your own or in community.

Why is Bible reading so vitally important in nurturing the life of faith? Why must we not allow it to be crowded out by other good things in life—including other reading we do?

Theologians make a distinction between general revelation and special revelation. The former is given to all and, as Matthew Barrett notes in an essay, "is broad (though far from empty) in what it says about God. This kind of revelation is found in creation and in every person's conscience."[5] Scripture has for centuries been understood as God's special revelation to us, "providing God's people with an enduring witness to the work of God in Christ."[6]

When I first held that lavishly illustrated children's Bible (in its largely unreadable, to me at the time, King James translation), I had never heard terms like "general" or "special" revelation. But even as a child, I sensed it was a special book; that it was something I should know about, spend time with. Years before I encountered the late novelist, pastor, and spiritual writer Frederick Buechner's words calling the Bible "a book about people who at one and the same time can be both believing and unbelieving, innocent and guilty, crusaders and crooks, full of hope and full of despair. In other words it is a book about us," I think I sensed that was so. That it was a book somehow, in some way, about me and about Christ, the one who came so that I might have life.

The Bible in One Hand, Resources in the Other

John R. W. Stott was a British pastor, Bible expositor, and author whose influence was felt throughout the evangelical world. He was known for many things, including dozens of books and commentaries including *Basic Christianity* and *The Cross of Christ* and for his work with the Lausanne Movement that mobilized global church leaders toward cooperation and reciprocity in learning and support. But

Stott was also known for his idea of "double listening," which he put forth in his book *The Contemporary Christian.* For Stott, "double listening" was the notion that we should continually have a Bible in one hand and a newspaper in the other. He was not implying they were equally authoritative in any way. Rather, he was suggesting that it was imperative that we connect the ancient, authoritative text to what is happening in the contemporary world. I think of Stott's "double listening" admonition when I ponder the process of reading Scripture as a spiritual discipline: That we keep the Bible in one hand, and reference works and commentaries in the other as one pathway to studying and applying Scripture.

In the entry on the Bible in his "theological ABC" titled *Wishful Thinking*, Frederick Buechner offered some helpful, practical guidance that was important to me as I was becoming a more serious reader of Scripture. He suggested that at least when we are new to reading the Bible, we not start at the beginning and attempt to read straight through to the end. "If you do, you're almost certain to bog down somewhere around the twenty-fifth chapter of Exodus," he writes. Instead, Buechner suggests what he calls the "high points" of the text, such as the Joseph stories in Genesis, the Job story, the Sermon on the Mount (Matthew 5–7), or Paul's letter to the Romans, especially chapter seven.[7] I would add reading the poetry of the Psalms and the wisdom of Proverbs.

Buechner also suggests having a good commentary with you as you approach your reading of the Bible to help illuminate the backgrounds and context. We are prone to read Scripture through the eyes of our own culture and experience, and commentaries, reference books, and other works can help us avoid misreading the text. Even though he was writing at a time prior to the explosion of modern translations and literary paraphrases like Eugene Peterson's *The Message,* he encouraged the reading of a variety of versions.

The guidance Buechner offered me decades ago proved helpful and still resonates with me today, in large measure. Commentaries and Bible background reference books that aid us in our understanding of the text are important. But other approaches to Scripture engagement have also shone a light on my path as the years have increased and as I've entered seasons that called for a reset.

Immersing Ourselves in Scripture

In particular, I have found the work of the Institute for Bible Reading and its "Immerse" methodology uncommonly helpful in my reading of Scripture as a spiritual discipline. Now a part of the Our Daily Bread organization, whose history dates back to the late 1930s, the IBR was founded to address what it called a "Bible disengagement epidemic."

"Our mission has its roots in the Bible publishing industry, where our team was confronted with sobering research that revealed two divergent trend lines," the IBR says in its literature. "Access to Bibles (especially in the West) is skyrocketing, but Bible engagement and Bible reading are in freefall. We have more Bibles than ever, yet there is a massive connection problem."[8]

To address that disconnection, Alex Goodwin in *The Bible Reset* and the staff of IBR in its work cast a vision for a new type of experience engaging with Scripture, inviting us to read the Bible at length without what they call "additives" (chapters and verses, study notes, and the like) and to invite others in that journey with us as on our own and in community with others we contemplate:

- What stood out to us in our reading?
- Was there anything troubling or confusing from the reading?
- Did anything we encountered make us think differently about God?
- And fundamentally, how might this reading impact how we live day to day?

"The goal of Bible reading is to understand the sacred writings in depth so we can learn to live them well," the editors of the *Immerse*

Reading Bible® write in the introduction to each volume in what they call "a sacred saga" built around the Bible's "drama in six acts."

The IBR has suggested that three bad habits of Bible reading have impacted our ability to engage Scripture well.

First, we read the Bible in small fragments, or "snack" on it rather than reading larger portions. Additionally, we read without understanding the context and fail to put ourselves firmly into the history being characterized in the text. And finally, we read only in isolation—we read as a "solo sport"—rather than considering the text in community, as well.

In entering the Immerse Bible experience, my Scripture engagement has been more like reading a book than ever before. Reading larger portions of Scripture around six clusters of the text organized as *Beginnings, Kingdoms, Prophets, Poets, Chronicles,* and *Messiah* has been illuminating and brought the text to life in fresh ways. I have found myself lost (in a good way) in the story of Scripture—its grand narrative, from its beginnings through its rich history and poetic books and the ultimate drama in the life of Christ.

To Snack or Not to Snack?

However, in addition to approaching Scripture in both a "double listening" and an "immersive" way, I continue to find value and insight in what some might consider as "snacking"—that is, books comprising liturgies that include Scripture text, prayers, and questions for reflection, or short portions of Scripture gleaned from a podcast or an audiobook edition of the Bible. In seasons when I find it difficult to spend more lengthy time in Scripture (or with a newspaper), reading liturgical books tethers me to the faith and allows a rhythm of engagement to be maintained.

In my church tradition, we receive the Eucharist each week, and I've often said that if I go more than one week without returning to the communion rail, kneeling and receiving the elements, I notice that. I sense the absence of hearing the Gospel, confessing my sins, and hearing the proclamation, "In Christ, you are forgiven." Those weekly trips to the communion rail are a fortifying reminder of who I am, in Christ.

In a similar way, going any length of time without engagement with Scripture via one pathway or another has a noticeable effect. I feel that absence. I am called back to the text, just as I am to the bread and wine. Books that combine a Scripture text, devotional readings, and prayers around a common theme serve to bring such reminders even when the pace of a given day or week has not allowed a more immersive reading experience.

The Bible and Journaling

A final way I've experienced more reflective and sustained engagement with Scripture is through the discipline of journaling as I read Scripture or listen to passages from the Old Testament, the Psalms, the Gospels, or other New Testament texts read aloud as part of the liturgy in worship services.

In her book *Journal Keeping*, Luann Budd suggests that journaling is a way we can "walk into the Scriptures," drawing on the words of 2 Timothy 2:7—"Think over what I say, for the Lord will give you understanding in all things" (NRSVue).[9] As we read and journal, we are apt to be more focused on what we encounter on the page, and we make note of questions or observations that arise within our hearts and minds. For me, the very act of putting a pen to paper and capturing words in response to a text heightens my engagement with Scripture, just as it does in walks in the natural world or in response to a profound work of poetry or fiction I am reading. I make notes of what stands out to me or what questions the words prompt. At times, I beg to differ with a promise that seems so certain in the text but so absent in my lived experience. At other times, I acknowledge God's presence and give thanks for it.

"We write in our journal as we approach, to assess our stance to the text," Budd writes. "We also write to ruminate on the truths we encounter. Writing gives us time to think deeply about an idea, seeing it from many vantage points while it settles into our heart."[10]

Recognizing the merged disciplines of Bible reading and journaling, in recent years some publishers have produced portions of Scripture (the Gospel of John, the Psalms, and Romans are three examples I have used) with interior pages designed to allow the reader to capture responses, write questions, or journal prayers in response to the text. Even if journaling has not been a discipline you have regularly practiced, consider picking up one of these portions and see whether or not this is, for you as it has been for me, a way of "walking into the Scriptures."

The Grand Drama of Scripture

There is not a single pathway to reading the Bible as a spiritual discipline and in a deeply engaged way. My experience suggests that different seasons of our lives call for unique paths of engagement. But the grand drama of Scripture is one we are wise to stay in tune with.

Near the conclusion of his book *The Bible Reset,* Alex Goodwin captures the importance of both the text and our engagement with it when he reminds us, "When we live into the Bible's story, centered on Christ, we see that the story comes full circle—that God's intentions to live on earth with his image bearers will not be thwarted, that sin and evil and death will not have the final say. All creation is groaning for this vision to be realized."[11]

That is the grand drama we encounter in Scripture. That is a story worth spending time with.

On Reading Scripture As a Spiritual Discipline

> The attitude one brings to reading the Bible profoundly influences what you get out of it. A lightbulb moment for me was when I read Saint Augustine's treatise *On Christian Doctrine*. There he said, "If you have an unshakable hold on faith, hope and love, you do not even need scripture except for the instruction of others." Augustine's description of the Bible as primarily there to help people grow in faith, hope and love puts the practice of scripture reading in a pragmatic and powerful perspective. When we read it with the intention of growing in faith, hope and love, the Holy Spirit can use our reading in transformative ways."
>
> —**Gregory S. Clapper**, author of *As If the Heart Mattered*

Reading Scripture as a Spiritual Discipline

15 Recommended Books

Below is a list of fifteen books that help guide us in reading, understanding, and applying the Bible with consistency and insight.

- *The Bible Reset*, by Alex Goodwin
- *Reading While Black: African American Biblical Interpretation as an Exercise in Hope*, by Esau McCaulley
- *How to Read the Bible for All Its Worth*, by Gordon D. Fee and Douglas Stuart
- *Ancient Christian Devotional* (series of three tied to lectionary cycles A, B, and C), general editor Thomas Oden, edited by Cindy Crosby

- *Saving the Bible from Ourselves: Learning to Read and Live the Bible Well*, by Glenn R. Paauw
- *Handbook for Personal Bible Study*, by William W. Klein
- *In the Lord I Take Refuge: 150 Daily Devotions through the Psalms*, by Dane Ortlund
- *Sacred Questions: A Transformative Journey through the Bible*, by Kellye Fabian
- *Immerse: The Reading Bible®*, Institute for Bible Reading/Tyndale House Publishers
- *The IVP Bible Background Commentary—Old Testament*, by John Walton, Victor Matthews, and Mark Chavalas
- *The IVP Bible Background Commentary—New Testament*, by Craig Keener
- *The Divine Hours*, edited by Phyllis Tickle (volumes for each of the lectionary cycles A, B, and C)
- *Design for Discipleship Bible Studies*, a series of seven studies for readers new to Scripture and the Christian life
- *Reading the Bible Latinamente*, by Ruth Padilla DeBorst, M. Daniel Carroll, and Miguel G. Echevarria
- *Bearing God's Name: Why Sinai Still Matters*, by Carmen Joy Imes

Part Two
The Wide, Wide, Wonderful World of Reading

"Seed-planting Dostoevsky: six seed-novels sit on a shelf in my study, all that is left of his life still making a difference in my life. God and passion. He spurned the trivial and went for the jugular."

—Eugene Peterson, from *Reality and the Vision*[1]

Chapter Four
THE POWER OF STORY: READING FICTION

"It's lies. All lies! You wrap your fiction in lies!" the woman bellowed out from the back of the auditorium as we began a panel discussion on the topic of "the power of story." She arrested the attention of the young, inexperienced moderator and his literary panelists, if not the entire audience.

The setting was an auditorium in the Jacob Javits Center in New York City during an American Booksellers Association Convention event that attracted thousands to the city to transact business with authors, agents, retailers, and other publishers from around the world.

The panel featured distinguished novelists of the day including Father Joseph Girzone, whose *Joshua* was appearing on bestseller lists; Calvin Miller, author of *The Singer Trilogy;* Dan Wakefield, a celebrated writer of fiction who had just released his spiritual memoir *The Returning;* and Walter Wangerin Jr., a pastor and writer of both fiction and nonfiction.

Wangerin, author of the National Book Award-winning *The Book of the Dun Cow* and other novels and short stories, sat to my immediate left as part of the panel. I was a young bookseller and the moderator of the panel that day, facing a disruption for which I had not prepared.

"It's lies! All lies! You wrap lies in fiction!"

Though we did not know each other well, Walt Wangerin and I both hailed from the midwestern state of Indiana, and we'd occasionally had conversations at bookselling and publishing events. I recall one memorable occasion together in the mountains above Boulder, Colorado, when Wangerin delivered a homily and presided over the Eucharist for a small gathering of booksellers that I was a part of.

But on this day in New York, he was one of several people I had invited to make remarks about the power of stories as drivers in our lives; the power of story in published books, especially in fiction. And he was decidedly not among the best known of our panelists.

But he was quick on his feet. And he was uncommonly wise. I remember looking toward where Walter sat. We made eye contact.

The woman standing in the back and addressing us all was from Australia, and she was reacting to a bestselling novel of the day that put her country's Aboriginal people in a poor and unjust light. Standing slowly, unfurling like an accordion file, Wangerin stroked his beard in a professorial, pastoral way befitting the English instructor and ordained Lutheran minister he was. With a very calm voice he responded with a request: "Please tell us what makes you say it's all lies. We want to understand."

His eyes never left her as she continued to speak with passion and conviction, with anger and resolve, expounding on her reasons for the belief that the novelist had told lies.

With arms crossed around his chest, as if giving himself—and her—a hug, Wangerin spoke once again after the woman ended her words of grievance.

"I don't know of the novel you're speaking about. *But you are right.* Novelists can tell or perpetuate lies, and we must be called to account when we do that," he told her, as if she were the only person in the room. "Thank you for your courage in speaking up. I know that my friends gathered here on this platform would never wish to do that. So, thank you. *We hear you.* We are sorry for your pain."

Walter Wangerin Jr., sat down. Silence descended. I returned to my opening remarks, with, I highly suspect, trembling knees and a quivering voice.

I don't remember anything else the novelists said at that day's conversation with the panelists on the power of story. I do remember Walt's words to that Australian woman, as if they were spoken just yesterday. And more than the words, I remember his empathy. I remember his kindness. I remember his gaze on a woman filled with anger, with pain. I remember how he consoled her, at some fifty or sixty yards across a convention center room. I've never forgotten it. Never forgotten his kindness, his empathy. I hope I never will.

This has become, ironically, a portrait of the power of story. An object lesson about why reading stories is not simply a means of obtaining a blissful distraction or escape from the cares of our world, but for the spiritual insight, companionship, and empathy they offer. I've carried it as a reminder of the sacred work of those who write and publish novels.

Why Read Fiction?

In a recent *Harvard Business Review* article titled "The Case for Reading Fiction," Christine Seifert draws on several fields of research including neuroscience as she posits that reading literary fiction aids people in developing emotional intelligence, empathy, theory of mind, and critical thinking—all characteristics that companies desire to see in the employees they recruit and retain.

"Research suggests that reading literary fiction is an effective way to enhance the brain's ability to keep an open mind while processing information, a necessary skill for effective decision-making," Seifert writes. Further, she asserts that skills such as "self-discipline, self-awareness, creative problem-solving, empathy, learning agility, adaptiveness, flexibility, positivity, rational judgment, generosity, and kindness" can be catalyzed through thoughtful reading of fiction.[2]

There was a time, long ago, when I likely would have taken issue with Seifert's conclusions. Like others, I believed that reading was an act of information gathering. Its value was landing with firm answers, building a solid knowledge base. The quickest route to that payoff, I believed, was through nonfiction.

The reading of Fyodor Dostoevsky's novel *The Brothers Karamazov*, first published in Russian in 1880, changed that equation forever. Though he wrote other novels destined to be called classics of literature, including *Crime and Punishment* and *The Idiot*, it was Dostoevsky's final novel in which he wrestled most powerfully with eternal questions of God's presence, God's absence, morality, suffering, and more.

I distinctly remember encountering the "Grand Inquisitor" section of the novel, words that literary critics have called the spiritual center of that book, late at night and weeping almost uncontrollably as I did so. My newborn son was sleeping in his bassinet just a few feet away. With equal portions of concern for me and worry that our child might be stirred from his own sleep, my wife awakened and whispered, "What's wrong? Are you alright?" It was hard to explain at that time the force, the impact, the *power* the novel had, and it is no less of a challenge today.

It's the power of story.

For a time, I inhabited Dostoevsky's world, his haunting questions, his piercing honesty, his exploration of family dynamics, of betrayal. I came in contact with the twin examples of the aged Father Zossima and the young, heroic protagonist Alyosha, whose ideals I wanted to embody in some small way in my life as a young father.

Writing in the introduction to a new translation of the work, Jon Surgal said that it was in *The Brothers Karamazov* that Dostoevsky dealt for the first and only time with the deaths of his father and his three-year-old son Alyosha, after whom the character in the novel is named. Just a month after the young son died, Surgal wrote, the novelist made a pilgrimage to Optina Pustyn, a Russian Orthodox monastery south of Moscow which was also used for spiritual retreats by the famed novelist Leo Tolstoy. On his return from the pilgrimage, Dostoyevsky began to write his masterpiece.

"Dostoyevsky was a God-possessed man if ever there was one, as is clear in everything he wrote and in every character he created," the esteemed British journalist Malcolm Muggeridge has written. "All his life he was questing for God, and found him only at the end of his days after passing through what he called 'the hell-fire of doubt.' Freedom to choose between good and evil he saw as the very essence of earthly existence."[3]

From Classic to Contemporary

Although *The Brothers Karamazov* is appropriately considered one of the classics of literature, the examples of the profound power of story neither begin nor end there. Contemporary writers carry on the tradition of exploring eternal questions in their own way, in their own times.

My encounter with Dostoevsky's work changed my mind about the value of literary fiction, and it sent me down a fresh path of reading as a spiritual discipline that incorporated voices from the genre of fiction past and present: William Kent Krueger and Kent Haruf; Jan Karon and Vinita Hampton Wright; Victor Hugo and Leo Tolstoy; Amanda Dykes and Amanda Cox; Sarah Loudin Thomas and Chris Fabry; Amor Towles and Patricia Raybon; Sandra Cisneros and Frederick Buechner; Erin Bartels and Toni Morrison; Shusaku Endo and Marilynne Robinson; Chaim Potok, and a late-arrival appreciation for John Steinbeck's *East of Eden*.

And there have been many others.

What these writers, each and all of them, have in common is the ability to paint a compelling, invitational canvas with a palette of words. They create a setting, a cast of characters, and believable lives and plot lines. They offer perspectives distinct from the reader's own and yet simultaneously provide companionship, light, life, hope. And the best of these novels do, in some way, in some measure, change our lives.

Our job is to show up as readers, to be attentive, to step into those worlds and consider what is to be seen, pondered, entered into on that canvas.

The Reality, and The Vision

In a collection of essays edited by Philip Yancey and published in the book *Reality and the Vision*, contemporary literary voices of note were asked to reflect on the writer who most stimulated their thinking, who unlocked their creative passion, and who changed their lives in significant ways. A common characteristic of those profiled, Yancey said, was that they portrayed the "sober reality of the human condition, and they also offer at least a glimpse of vision that inspires hope."[4]

Of the 17 chapters featured in the book, nine of the writers who were paid such tribute were novelists or writers of children's tales: Hans Christian Andersen, J. R. R. Tolkien, Flannery O'Connor, Ray Bradbury, George MacDonald, Leo Tolstoy, Aleksandr Solzhenitsyn, Evelyn Waugh, and Dostoevsky.

I think this is instructive of the power of story, and the value of incorporating fiction as part of our spiritual discipline or practice of reading.

Writing in the book's preface, Yancey said that "the fantasists, such as Tolkien, Bradbury, and MacDonald, create a new reality that sends echo waves back to this one. The reader who lives through 1500 pages of suspense and tension and darkness in Tolkien's great trilogy may well feel, at the moment when the spell of evil breaks and the darkness of Mordor lifts, a gust of glory and freedom and light; an encounter with 'joy beyond the walls of the world more poignant than grief,' in Tolkien's own words."[5]

The book served as something of a record of what the contemporary writers like Yancey, Wangerin, Madeleine L'Engle, Richard Foster, Eugene Peterson, and others felt were among the books that should be passed on. Books "across time and generations" that "carry the thoughts, and feelings, the essence, of the human spirit."[6]

During the pandemic that shook the world beginning in early 2020, for months I uncharacteristically found myself unable to read nonfiction or even most of the Bible, save for the book of Psalms. When I tried to do so, it was as if my soul cried out for rest from the cares, stresses, and pain of the world.

But novels were another story.

Works of fiction transported me away from the intensity of those months of reports on infection rates, hospitalizations, mortalities, school closings, and mask mandates and took me through a veil into another time and another place—a town like the fictitious Holt, Colorado, imagined by the late novelist Kent Haruf in his books including, most notably, *Plainsong*, *Eventide*, and *Benediction*, and his posthumously published final work, *Our Souls at Night.*

In an essay on fiction in his annotated list of spiritual reading titled *Take and Read*, Eugene Peterson writes, "Novelists work the same field in which Christians pray, believe, and obey, plowing and sowing and harvesting all the interconnections of ordinary lives. . . . Anyone, I think, serious about (the) elemental conditions of story, person, and place in which our salvation is worked out will welcome novelists as friends, and seek to spend time in their company."[7]

For several months during the pandemic when kindness and decency were sorely lacking in each evening's newscasts and our political and social discourse, Kent Haruf became one of the primary writers who accompanied and sustained me as I read or in some cases reread his novels, which elevate and make compelling the simple act of decency. Literary critics often say that it is harder to write about characters who are good than about those who are evil. Haruf had an unusual gift to portray goodness in ways that prompt readers to want to know (and be more like) the likes of Harold and Raymond McPherson, the Holt, Colorado, farmers who take in the pregnant and unmarried teenager Victoria Roubideaux. The McPherson brothers give her not only a home over her head, but acceptance, love, and security, while sheltering her from the small-town arrows of judgment as much as possible. Although Haruf had written for much of his life with little recognition, including the novels *The Tie That Binds* and *Where You Once Belonged*, it was not until *Plainsong*, published when he was 56, that he drew critical praise, including being a finalist for the National Book Award.

According to his obituary in *The New York Times,* Haruf had the unusual practice of pulling a wool hat over his eyes as he sat down each morning at his manual typewriter to work on his novel "so he could 'write blind,' fully immersing himself in the fictitious small town in eastern Colorado where he set a series of quiet, acclaimed novels." He believed doing so took away the terror of writing sentences, and chapters, and ultimately the stories themselves, because when you're writing blind "you can't go back and rewrite a sentence. It calls for storytelling, not polishing."[8]

Reading Haruf's novels challenged me in those dark days of 2020 to seek to metaphorically write a story of decency and truth and goodness through the chapters of my own life and work and engagement in the world, even in the midst of its discord.

That is the power of story.

Finding New Voices

Like many of you, I'm sure, I love a good beach read. David Baldacci's thrillers are one of my guilty pleasures. Classic stories like *The Count of Monte Cristo* or children's books like *The Secret Garden* that I missed as a young person are often tucked in my bag as I go. John Grisham's legal adventures and even an occasional Nicholas Sparks romance may also find their way down to the surf and sand, even if I may be tempted to take off the dust jacket of the latter's books in an effort to preserve a sense of being a reader of more serious books!

But I'm always on the lookout for the work of novelists past and present that I believe should be handed down to the next generation—books like John Steinbeck's *East of Eden,* that are still going to be read generations from now. I make it a practice, when I meet new people or enjoy a cup of tea with an old friend, to always ask, "What are you reading?" and I give them time to ponder the question and offer a response. Especially if the person comes from a different culture, ethnic group, or part of the world, I'm eager to know what they are encountering, how the books are shaping them, and what they believe is ripe for my own consideration.

Attending literary events in your community—whether at bookstores or libraries or other contexts—is another way to be introduced to new literary voices.

As with reading all other genres and reading in the seasons of life covered later in this book, maintain a posture of curiosity, openness, and engagement. A world of wonders awaits us all.

Wise, Whispering Companions

The late Walter Wangerin Jr. came to my rescue that day in New York City long ago when we as a panel were confronted by the pain caused by a novelization of the story of Aboriginal people in Australia. That experience bound me to his literary output—both fiction and non-fiction, for the rest of his writing life. Books like *The Crying for the Vision, Miz Lil and the Chronicles of Grace*, and *Ragman and Other Cries of Faith* occupied a special residence in my heart and mind then, as they do today.

Wangerin considered the children's tales of Hans Christian Andersen to be his most important literary influence, a pictureless gift his father had given him as a young child and read to him when what he most needed was companionship.

"Hans Andersen's stories, though simple on the surface, contain a precise and tender perception of personal development. They are honest about the hard encounter of the 'real world'—honest about evil and the tendency to evil in each of us," Wangerin wrote of those stories. "Andersen did not coddle me, the 'me' who was revealed in his fairy tales. He didn't sweeten the bitter facts which I already knew regarding myself. But he offered me hope, for in his tales even when evil has been chosen, forgiveness may follow—therein lies extraordinary hope."[9]

Perhaps that is the power of reading fiction as part of our spiritual disciplines. Another avenue for encountering the age-old, life-changing narrative of creation, fall, and redemption—and the hope therein.

~

The Power of Story: Reading Fiction

> "Tell me a story" is probably one the first pleas we make as a child beyond requests for our physical needs. To sit on a beloved parent's lap or at the feet of a teacher and be told a story delights us. To learn to read stories on our own is amazing. Alas, it's a joy we too often put aside as we age and "put away (supposedly) childish things." That's a real loss, I believe. We live by stories. We tell them to each other all the time.
>
> The power of story, I believe (as someone primarily known for writing nonfiction), is that it invites us into a world of possibility and wonder. As the characters come alive and wrestle with their trials and triumphs, we grow and stretch and learn. That's because fiction can say things such that we can receive them in a way that we can't in a nonfiction book. We accept the truth—or at least wrestle with it—in a way we won't often in a nonfiction book. We need fiction. "Tell me a story."
>
> **—J. Brent Bill**, author of *Holy Silence: The Gift of Quaker Spirituality*, *Amity: Stories from the Heartland*, and others.

The Power of Story: Reading Fiction

15 Recommended Works of Fiction

Below is a list of a dozen novels of deep impact from my own practice of reading as a spiritual discipline. As I look at my list, I note that most if not all probe to some degree the darker realities of the human experience, but most also simultaneously shed light in the midst of darkness.

- *The Brothers Karamazov*, by Fyodor Dostoyevsky
- *Ordinary Grace*, by William Kent Krueger
- *The Unhiding of Elijah Campbell*, by Kelly Flanagan
- *The Gift of Asher Lev*, by Chaim Potok
- *The Edge of Belonging*, by Amanda Cox
- *Grace at Bender Springs*, by Vinita Hampton Wright
- *Ashes*, by Christopher de Vinck
- *Amity: Stories from the Heartland*, by J. Brent Bill
- *The Thanatos Syndrome*, by Walker Percy
- *All the Light We Cannot See*, by Anthony Doerr
- *By Paths Untrodden*, by James K. Honig
- *Born of Gilded Mountains*, by Amanda Dykes
- *Plainsong*, by Kent Haruf
- *I Cheerfully Refuse*, by Leif Enger
- *East of Eden*, by John Steinbeck

"Reading, you turn a page to a poem you haven't encountered before. Think of this poem as a bare table, well lighted, with darkness all around. It's your table; each reader has his or her own."

—Ted Kooser, *The Poetry Home Repair Manual*[1]

Chapter Five
The Power of Paying Attention: Reading Poetry

It was a breezy, cool-but-not-yet-cold autumn day with dark rain clouds gathering on the western horizon. My wife and I had traveled 90 miles from our suburban home to hike the Harlem Hills Prairie, situated in northern Illinois not far from the Wisconsin border, to what is known as a remnant (not planted) prairie, the landscape of our state's past.

The Illinois Department of Natural Resources, which helps manage the nearly 100-acre plot, touts it as the area's largest and finest remaining gravel hill prairie and heralds the inclusion of several threatened or endangered species of plants that once would have flourished in the rich Illinois soil prior to the development of highways, housing subdivisions, and mass, mono-crop agriculture. Even though we were past the season where the subtle but celebrated pasque flowers or the showy pale purple coneflower would be on stage in all their splendor, nonetheless the prairie riveted our attention, made us focus on the life and beauty all around us, and caused us to slow down for an afternoon and simply *be.*

The impact was a lot like my experience of reading poetry.

As I walked along the trail that looped up, over, and around the rolling prairie, I was struck by the similarities between spending time in the natural world—especially a place like Harlem Hills, which is now as it has been for centuries—and the reading, reflecting, and dwelling on works of poetry. We slow down. We ponder. We focus on beauty. We consider the meaning to be found in it, apart from any utilitarian purpose. Our attention is heightened. We are present in unique ways.

Poetry, a Universal Language

A textbook titled *Sound and Sense: An Introduction to Poetry* is one of the enduring guides to teaching students to both write and appreciate poetry. In its pages, Laurence Perrine and Thomas R. Arb speak of poetry being as universal as language—and nearly as ancient.

"The most primitive peoples have used it, and the most civilized have cultivated it. In all ages and in all countries, poetry has been written, and eagerly read or listened to, by all kinds and conditions of people—by soldiers, statesmen, lawyers, farmers, doctors, scientists, clergy, philosophers, kings, and queens," they write. Poetry, they say, "has been regarded as something central to existence, something having unique value to the fully realized life, something that we are better off for having and without which we are spiritually impoverished."[2]

On January 20, 2021, just two weeks after the assault on the United States capital following a contentious presidential cycle and unsubstantiated claims of a stolen election, a young woman named Amanda Gorman stepped to the dais and read a presidential inaugural poem titled "The Hill We Climb." At the age of 22, she was the youngest inaugural poet in US history, and she delivered in just 723 words a powerful, poetic message on unity, collaboration, and togetherness. I remember watching it live, at once mesmerized by her yellow jacket, her voice, her bright red hairband, and most of all her words about rebuilding and reconciling; about being paradoxically battered and brave and beautiful all at once. For a period of time thereafter, the poem was lodged in the memory if not on the lips of millions of people in our nation, and undoubtedly many others looking on from other parts of the world. We stopped. We paid attention in the midst of our trauma. We dreamed of a better way, a better day.

Poetry. Beauty. The power of words.

In the immediate aftermath of that inauguration, poetry had one of its best ambassadors in Amanda Gorman. Sales of the gift edition of *The Hill We Climb* and her subsequent collection *Call Us What We Carry* placed poetry books on the *New York Times* bestseller list, not an everyday occurrence for books in this genre.

Where Does Our Love of Poetry Go?

In the small, independent bookstore my wife and I operated, we devoted one four-foot section to poetry even though it was the least-traveled section in our store. We kept it there as a matter of principle, believing that exposure to works of poetry was central to our mission. Poetry collections by Luci Shaw, John Donne, Wendell Berry, John Leax, Walter Wangerin Jr., and Calvin Miller were there, alongside many others, both classic and contemporary. If we were still operating that store today we would no doubt add voices like Maya Angelou, Mary Oliver, Denise Levertov, Christian Wiman, Ted Kooser, and Amanda Gorman, among others.

Many children are taught haiku poetry and delight in sharing it with others. We love poetry set to music in short songs, the words and rhythms stirring deep reflection within us.

Where does that love go? Why do so many of us so often set it aside? Why do we not more regularly incorporate poetry in our reading as a spiritual discipline beyond, perhaps, our reading of the biblical books of Job, Psalms, Proverbs, Ecclesiastes, and the Song of Solomon? When we are exposed to poetry done well, and given time to reflect, as we did with Amanda Gorman in January of 2021, we *feel* something, *sense* something important has just happened. The form of writing slows down the pace of our reading and often prompts rereading the words on the page and dwelling on them.

At a spiritual formation conference in Wichita, Kansas, some years ago, I had the occasion to lead a reading of a poem by the Irish mystic, poet, and priest John O'Donohue in *lectio divina* style—slowly, repeatedly. We read in different voices, with people who gathered each taking their turn. The poem, "For Longing," provoked deep contemplation. And, in turn, heartfelt responses. I was struck by how very different the observations were, how different words and phrases stood out to each person, and how the meaning they made out of the close reading of the poem was personal.

The Power of Paying Attention: An Example

In my mind, Ted Kooser is among the very finest poets writing today. Although he is associated with the prairies and plains of Nebraska, where he has lived and taught for decades, the Pulitzer Prize-winning poet was born in Iowa.

Of all of his poetry, it is his "Estate Sale" from his book *Splitting An Order* that has come to symbolize the power of poetry to both express a life lived with attentiveness, and to call a reader's life to do the same.

As you read, perhaps even with a journal and pen in hand, allow Kooser's words in the poem below to paint a picture for you. Allow it to call you to attention, and consider what he is seeing on that farm on a plains state in the midwestern part of the United States. What do you see? What do you hear? What do you feel? What do you smell? What do you *remember* from your own life, and estate sales you may have gone to or imagined?

Ted Kooser, "Estate Sale"[3]

At a broken window, an old cobweb
wadded and rolled by the wind:
one of those long woolen stockings
your grandmother wore.

The parts of a broken birdfeeder,
put into a box for fixing later,
the lid warped on its hinges,
its tiny white feathers of paint
loose to the touch, one of the side boards
split—but the pieces saved, the board
where the birds sat down to eat
now rotted and black from the rains.
In the slot where the glass once fit,
a few seeds missed by the mice,
some of them sprouted but dead now,
the pale wings stiffly folded.

An empty coffee can
wrapped in aluminum foil.
In this poor urn, the peonies
rode to their graveyard,
covering their faces
with immaculate gloves.

A baseball with one of its seams
split wide, its skin
mottled and green, a planet
with one of its mountain ranges
blown open, displaying
a kind of universe, electrons
spinning, leaving their vapor trails.

The nest of some tiny bird,
each blade of dead grass
spun into its place
on the potter's wheel
of her busy movements,
preparing a vessel for song.

A soggy shoe box, and in its grayness
a yellow tin of corn pads rising
sun-like over the reflecting pools
of a neatly folded pair of glasses.

In its tattered paper sleeve,
a 78-rpm record, Blue Label
with dog and Victrola,
dust sealing the grooves.
If we had the means to play it,
Over the music we'd hear
The rhythmical cough
of a woman who once
bent toward the turning disc
and tried to sing along.

Clipped into a sleeve of waxed paper,
a lock of hair tied with a ribbon
the color of water, the hair too yellow
to have been real, but perhaps, when
left to itself like the colors in memories
grown brighter with time.

A windup wristwatch
with a cracked leather band:
throughout his life, a man
may out of curiosity

push his hand up to the wrist
through a hole in the fence
of time, and then, one day
as he leans there enjoying the hours, someone comes up
on the other side, takes hold,
and pulls him through.

The red, webbed collar for a dog,
bristled and frayed to a foamy white
where it bit back hard at the buckle.

A section of unused stovepipe
standing unsnapped and open
like somebody's coat, and in it
the thin blue smoke of a spiderweb.

Five or six feet of heavy black
electrical wire gathered up into a few loose coils like a lariat,
the last few inches of each end
brought over and under the coils
and then very carefully twisted
into a tight little pigtail,
the tarry insulation drawing back
from neat, clean cuts that let
the inner wires—white, black,
and the bright green ground—
push out of the darkness
like the first shoots of a lily,
smooth tubes through which
the tips of copper petals ease.

A 25-amp glass fuse.
Under the clear ice of its surface
it is easy to see the silver ribbon
of a motionless fish,
its body aligned with the current.

An envelope of dime-store
photo mounting corners—
little black bats that seem always to wait at the edges.

A bucket of white, coiled springs
from a rotten hammock,
each with the tight muscularity
of a living thing, drawn back
against itself, defensive,
every nerve tuned to a snarl.

A wooden cheese box with a blue horse
impressed in the side—big mare
in blinders, head lowered and pulling hard
at a wagon of cream cans. A man
in a hat with his face in blue shadow
up on the seat, reins loose in his hands.
The cheese box is easing its seams
under the load of a dozen burned-out
spark plugs, its thin brads loose
In their rusty holes, the side slats
split, the dead plugs tumbled together,
muscle to muscle, dark smears of oil
on their tight white letter-sweaters.

On a nail, a chain fish-stringer
with a few scales stuck to its open hooks.
Give it a shake and it whips and glitters
in muscular waves,
throwing off light like drops of water.

What can be read in the open book
of an old brass door hinge? Here are two
in a coffee can, one of them coated
with cream-colored paint and one brown,
the first from a door that once swung

into the kitchen and out, fanning
the fragrance of pot roast, its paint
worried and chipped; the other from
the cold brown door to the attic stairs
that was rarely opened, behind which stood
winter, wearing an old woolen coat
with mothballs loose in his pockets.
The first hinge swung smooth on a film
of black oil from bacon and chops;
the other cried out through the frost.

The wooden wheel in this old pulley
had nowhere to roll away to,
so it stayed right here in its iron harness,
whining and whining.

A folded wooden clotheshorse,
its creamy ribs like bone,
like a beach umbrella blown inside out
by the cold sea-wind of time,
and next to this, a galvanized tub
in which a washboard leans
like a staircase up into the present.

In a tin can, a packet of spinach seeds
folded over and paper-clipped,
with a neat hole chewed in the side
and the seeds all eaten but one;
a tiny brown leather valise
packed with green scarves.

A tire that was never used,
still wrapped in paper swaddling—
old road maps, maybe, soaked
and smoothed around it like poultices
to cool the lust for rolling.

A discarded billfold, its breathing
shallow a clam with a brown hinge
polished by wear, the halves
closed loosely over the flattened pearl
of a buffalo nickel.

And among these homely things,
an antique gilded harp,
its dusty strings like a curtain
drawn over the silence,
stroked by fingers of light.

When I first encountered this poem, I was utterly drawn in to the poet's words. I felt as if I were with Kooser on that Nebraska or Iowa farm where an estate sale of all of a family's belongings were out on display and available to the highest bidder. I saw the cobwebs, the coffee can, the split-seamed baseball. I saw the 78-rpm record and glass fuses that once gave light and power to the farmstead. I smelled the decay of the wood in the barn. I heard the sounds that the now-dusty stringed harp once made in the home's parlor before it was moved out for the sale.

The power of paying attention. Kooser, the poet, paid attention that day. And his readers, through the power of his poetry, can do the same.

Take a moment to reflect on your response to your reading of this poem. Perhaps try rereading it or look at your observations if you journaled. What did your heart and mind fasten their attention on? And what impact did that attentiveness have?

The reading of Kooser's poem, for me, was an exercise in paying attention, and that exercise has had an impact on all of the reading of poetry I have done since. His careful expression of words, his attention to detail, and his artful portrait of what he saw that day are an example to us all.

Caring for Words

In my reading as a spiritual discipline, I have encountered thousands of writers who care for words and their impact. But as I have grown in the reading of poetry as part of that discipline, I have come to believe that the poet has an extra measure of such care. Though Kooser's "Estate Sale" is a long poem, the poet is generally working with an economy of words, of space, when compared to the novelist or the nonfiction writer. This tends to sharpen and make more precise their use of words and phrases.

"Most people who care about words would say that poetry is the finest form of writing," Kathryn Lindskoog suggests in her book *Creative Writing: For Those Who Can't Not Write.*[4] She divides the genre into what she calls "art poetry" (serious poetry; that which literature professors and others take seriously) and "folk poetry." Art poetry is "what Robert Frost was talking about when he said that poetry takes life by the throat."[5] Folk poetry is, by contrast, "sometimes called greeting card verse. It's easy to read and understand. It has broad appeal."[6]

My early forays into poetry reading likely would have fallen into Lindskoog's "folk" category: Collections of poetry and songs published by Blue Mountain Arts and virtually resembling an over-sized greeting card. I still like pulling out the verse by Peter McWilliams, Max Ehrmann, Susan Polis Schutz, and others. But over time, I came to see the wisdom in setting aside more time for the "art poetry" of writers like Kooser, Maya Angelou, Denise Levertov, and Catherine de Vinck.

"A poem says, *Pay attention!* A poem brackets an experience and turns it upside down in order for us to see it right side up again," Jill Peláez Baumgaertner writes in *Taking Root in the Heart,* a collection of poems that were published by *The Christian Century.* "It surprises and upsets the usual. It uses rhythm and rhyme and all of the other sound effects the language provides . . . to bring into focus suffering or beauty or fear or God's compelling presence. Or absence, as the case may be. Poetry tackles the big questions, sometimes pointing to tentative answers, sometimes offering more questions."[7]

Baumgaertner is herself a poet, a professor, and something of an ambassador for this genre of writing and reading that helps us all powerfully pay attention. And over time, I, too, have come to be something of an "evangelist" for poets and poetry. And like others, I see the reading of and reflecting on poetry as something of a spiritual discipline in our hyper-connected, distracted world. But we do have to stop, slow down, and dwell on the words before us. And as we do, we may find connections between our reading of poetry and our practice of prayer.

"Poetry and prayer are closely related. Even poems that make no pretense of broaching the sacred invite us to look closely and listen to words, to notice how they trigger associations and invite the mind to play with meaning, how they summon feelings that take us by surprise," the poet and writer of nonfiction Marilyn McEntyre has written. "Poets slow us down. They teach us to stop and go in before we go on."[8]

Why Does God Keep Making Poets?

In a July 2023 column in the *New York Times*, opinion writer Tish Harrison Warren interviewed her former Washington University (St. Louis) poetry teacher Abram Van Engen, asking him to offer her readers instruction on how to read poetry. He shared with Warren his path to reading poetry through Gerard Manley Hopkins's "As Kingfishers Catch Fire," and then went on to the reason for what Warren called "the human urge for poetry."

Van Engen, author of the recent book *Word Made Fresh: An Invitation to Poetry for the Church*, told Warren, "One reason I think we keep making poetry is because we are ourselves poems. There's a verse in the Bible (Ephesians 2:10) in which we are described as the 'handiwork of God.' But it's the same Greek root that goes into the word 'poetry.' It means, 'a made thing.' A more literal translation is that we are, as human beings, the *poems* of God. So we keep making poetry because we are ourselves poems." Van Engen goes on to say, "I also think of poetry as the art of attention. It's the ability to pay attention to the world and produce for the world the name of something that must be known."[9]

Our lives are God's masterpieces, or God's *poiema* in Greek, and as such our lives are meant to be listened to because God is speaking into and through our lives. In my experience, it is through poetry and its close counterpart, songs, that we can be drawn to attentiveness and a discernment of what individual moments and extended seasons mean.

Speaking Into the Human Soul

Luci Shaw is a writer who has tutored me in a variety of capacities, first in her work as a publisher and later through her memoir of grief titled *God in the Dark*, which powerfully conveyed the story of her husband Harold's death and its impact on her life. But most of all, it is through her poems that Shaw has instructed and inspired me and heightened my attentiveness to my life in both its interior and exterior dimensions.

In a recent conversation, Shaw told me that she was first made aware of the power of poetry at a very early age. Later, as an adult, she "began to recognize the worldwide human impulse to sing and to speak into the air words composed in a form we call 'poetry,' a form different from story or exposition or instruction because of its ability to speak uniquely into the human soul, sparking imaginative insight and artistic appreciation."[10]

Shaw has been fostering such insight and appreciation for much of her 95 years. Her ability to pay attention and to call us to attention through words is evident in her poem "Poetry Workshop," written on Harvester Island in the Gulf of Alaska.

> All morning I struggle in the cabin,
> working to make words speak their
> essential truth, while all around me
> mountains and gales and untamed waters

speak without constraint. Gulls
wheel and cry and cluster on the spit
at will, and under the gray steel of the inlet
the Cohos and Pinks test the limits
of the seine before being drawn up into
the alien air, each telling a unique story.

Within the wooden walls
I endeavor to compose one perfect poem.[11]

~

Through her own writing and teaching, my wife has the opportunity to speak to a host of gatherings each year. As often as not, I go with her and never fail to learn and to be inspired. At virtually all of her classes or programs she ends by quoting a short portion of the poet Mary Oliver's poem "Yes! No!" from the book *White Pines: Poems and Prose Poems.* Oliver writes (and Cindy reminds her listeners), "To pay attention, this is our endless and proper work." That phrase has become ingrained in my own soul. And I believe that poetry and poets—people like Oliver, and Kooser; like McEntyre and Gorman; like Luci Shaw—help us pay attention. May I do so. May you do so. May we all do so, all the days of our lives.

Reading Poetry: The Power of Paying Attention

> Writing a poem requires of the writer a different approach than developing a novel or an essay. Poetry's deliberate focus pays attention to something that strikes the writer as unusual, beautiful, extraordinary, significant, unique—whether a season, an emotion, a relationship, an event, a landscape. This concept of "paying attention" is derived from the Latin *ad-tendere*, a *reaching toward*, or a *reaching into* human experience. It means examining or taking an event, a theme, or a focus and developing it imaginatively, discovering connections or relationships that urge and encourage us into creativity, in the composition of a poem, which is the reward for this focus of attention. Once the writing is completed, reading the poem aloud encourages us to investigate its rhythm and meaning.
>
> **Luci Shaw, author, poet,** *Polishing the Petoskey Stone*, *Angels Everywhere*, and *Eye of the Beholder*

The Power of Paying Attention: Reading Poetry

15 Recommended Works of Poetry

Below is a list of a poetry collections of impact from my own practice of reading as a spiritual discipline. Some are from explicitly Christian voices while others are not but illuminate our lives with words of beauty, searing questions, and deep ponderings. All of them help us to pay attention to our lives and to the world around us.

- *Eye of the Beholder: Poems*, by Luci Shaw
- *New Collected Poems*, by Wendell Berry

- *Splitting An Order*, by Ted Kooser
- *Donne: Poems and Prose*, by John Donne (Everyman's Library Pocket Poets)
- *Rilke: Poems*, by Rainer Maria Rilke (Everyman's Library Pocket Poets)
- *The Complete Collected Poems of Maya Angelou*, by Maya Angelou
- *Book of Mercy*, by Leonard Cohen
- *Home Going: Poetry for a Season*, by Carolyn Weber
- *Sea Glass: New & Selected Poems*, by Luci Shaw
- *Christian Poetry in America Since 1940: An Anthology*, edited by Micah Mattix and Sally Thomas
- *Call Us What We Carry*, by Amanda Gorman
- *Hammer Is the Prayer: Selected Poems*, by Christian Wiman
- *Journey to the Morning Light*, by Catherine de Vinck
- *Collected Poems 1974-2004*, by Rita Dove
- *Devotions: The Selected Poems of Mary Oliver*, by Mary Oliver

"I don't like to tell people what to take from my books. I prefer my readers interpret the words for themselves, to discover the themes and significance through their own reasoning with the information given. But if there is one thing readers take from this book, I hope it is that history matters. Stories matter, and it also matters who is telling these stories."

—Brandy Colbert, *Black Birds in the Sky*[1]

Chapter Six
The Power of Perspective: Reading Diverse Voices

The Southwest Airlines Boeing 737 aircraft touched down on the runway of the airport situated eight miles from my ultimate destination near the city center of Tulsa, Oklahoma. It was an unseasonably sweltering day in late May, the kind during which the flight attendants ask deplaning passengers to lower their window shades to keep the plane cool for the next passengers who will board.

I was in Tulsa not to see its heralded attractions such as the Bob Dylan Center, the Tulsa Botanic Garden, or the Church Studio built in 1972 by musician and Oklahoma native Leon Russell to house a recording operation for his Shelter Records company. Instead, I traveled to Tulsa on a quest to see the historic Greenwood district, an area that was burned virtually to the ground on May 31 and June 1, 1921, on what has come to be known as the Tulsa Race Massacre.

And I was here because of reading books that told that story—books that prompted me to try to understand the incomprehensible, to think more deeply about the unthinkable. I wanted to see what is there today, imagine what was there in 1921, and consider the story of Greenwood in light of a larger racial history of the United States, not simply in the South, but also throughout the country.

Books like *The Burning* by Tim Madigan, *Riot and Remembrance* by James Hirsch, *Built from the Fire* by Victor Luckerson, *Death in the Promised Land* by Scott Ellsworth, *Black Birds in the Sky* by Brandy Colbert, and *Requiem for the Massacre* by RJ Young all merged together to bring the largely unrecognized tragedy of 1921 Greenwood out into the open for me and in public discourse as we approached the centennial anniversary. These and other books about the Tulsa Race Massacre—the devastation of what was known as America's Black Wall Street and the considerable loss of not only property but Black lives—begged for a reckoning, a grappling with history that many of us would prefer to ignore.

Although in an imperfect and only partial way, books have the ability to help us experience history and understand our stories as people, as nations, as a world: racial, ethnic, gender, generational, even theological. To experience that impact, we must be committed to reading diverse voices and engaging with widely divergent topics as we grapple with dark chapters of our life together and divisions both historic and current—regardless of how uncomfortable we may feel.

As I walked on that hot day in May of 2014 through the John Hope Franklin Center for Reconciliation in Tulsa's Greenwood district and encountered historical photos and documents related to the massacre that is now more than a century past, I *did* feel uncomfortable. Questions like, "If I had been there on those days in 1921, what would I have done? Would I have participated in the injustice or fought against it? Would my privilege as a White person have caused me to stay silent at best, or participate in the destruction and death at worst?"

Yes, it felt uncomfortable, even contemplating my own answer, unknowable as it was. But I also felt grateful to be prompted to even ask the question. I also was grateful to encounter the power of perspective from the survivors, such as Olivia Hooker, Ernestine Gibbs, and Clarence Bruner, told through stories created by the John Hope Franklin Center.

Books were the portal, the doorway through which I walked—and you can walk, as well—toward perspective and understanding of the painful experiences that others endured.

A Need for Intentionality

As human persons, we are drawn to certain kinds of music or have a fondness for a particular type of architecture. We may favor a certain cuisine or, for those of us who attend church, a favored style or form of worship. Without intentionality, we are prone to forming relationships primarily with people in a common socio-economic background or a shared ethnic identity. Without a great deal of effort and focus, our churches can be quite homogeneous, not reflecting God's beautiful mosaic but just one pattern of that tapestry, even if we are in a city or town with a diverse population, as is increasingly true in many areas of the world, both urban and suburban, cities and towns.

As readers, we can also be drawn to a narrow set of voices, topics, and theological traditions. At worst, our reading can be designed (without knowing it, perhaps) to simply reinforce our existing beliefs and not consider alternative points of view. Echo chambers not only are present in our nightly news or preferred social media channels, but can exist in our book reading as well.

As we seek to cultivate the spiritual discipline of reading, we will be well served by intentionally seeking out voices who may be unfamiliar, perspectives that may be uncomfortable, and theological or religious traditions that may seem foreign to us. Doing so helps us build bridges and open windows of understanding.

Building Bridges

I've always been fascinated by bridges, their architecture and the way in which they carry us from one side of a gulf or chasm to another—sometimes large, other times small. The Golden Gate Bridge in San Francisco is, of course, among the crown jewels of them all. The bridge over Lake Pontchartrain in Louisiana is another memorable one, though not due to its design but rather its length: 24 miles. The Sydney Harbour Bridge in Australia and the Brooklyn Bridge in New York are other marvels that I have enjoyed seeing up close and studying, for both their architecture and their splendid history.

Even as a young boy living in the Midwest who rarely traveled outside of Indiana, I always noticed bridges and loved going over them, peering below at rivers, creeks, or railroad beds. One in particular stands out from those days. It was an arched steel bridge painted a vivid green that I would travel across regularly on trips from our house to a family member's just outside of a neighboring town. I loved being able to see the water running under either side of the bridge, with canoeists sometimes visible. I loved its color, its sturdy design, and the sure sense of safety (even as a small child) that it would get me from one side of the river to the other.

I have found books to be bridges of understanding in some of the areas of human discourse fraught with challenges: race, ethnicity, gender, socio-economic disparities, theological traditions, generational dynamics, and more. But we have to be intentional about this type of reading. It doesn't just happen. This reading needs to be born out of a commitment to empathy and valuing listening to voices and stories that are not at all like our own.

The season I spent reading books about the Tulsa Race Massacre didn't only shed light on a single historical event, but it also opened up powerful perspectives on a much wider lens of injustice that occurred in other cities not only in the 1920s but also down to the present day. Similarly, reading biographies of the Latin American martyr Oscar Romero and studying his own works, including *The Violence of Love*, shed light on the experiences of brothers and sisters in Christ in Latin America. Reading Roman Catholic spirituality and theological writers fostered an understanding when a member of our family was received into that church, and reading Father Kallistos Ware's *The Orthodox Way* and Andrew Louth's *Introducing Eastern Orthodox Christianity* built the same bridges when another member was chrismated and welcomed into an Orthodox church parish.

A disciplined reading of female authors has long been a part of my commitment, as well, born out of a belief that women have unique perspectives, gifts, and stories that are important not only for other women but also for men like me to encounter. Reading authors like Kate Bowler, Wendy Murray, Barbara Brown Taylor, Marilyn McEntyre, Maya Angelou, Luci Shaw, Phyllis Tickle, Marlena Graves, Susan Cain, and Joan Chittister are representative of this. My life would be impoverished had I not encountered the work of each and every one of them.

Indeed, during a season of tremendous struggle vocationally and spiritually, McEntyre's *Word by Word: A Daily Spiritual Practice* was a singular source of comfort, reassurance, and guidance. Her weekly series of meditations on themes of listening, receiving, enjoying, letting go, being still, and more provided a sense of quiet reassurance that, in the words of Julian of Norwich, "All will be well. All manner of things will be well." McEntyre's was a voice I needed to hear and respond to. And she was there in the pages of a book.

Learning from Younger/Older Generations

I've long been a lover of diverse styles of music—whether jazz, classical, folk, pop, rock, blues, they have all been important to me. But as I've gotten older I confess that staying abreast of and open to the musical styles produced by younger generations has been a stretch. Hyperpop, rage rap, pop punk, and other current genres and trends in music being released by young artists typically leave me reaching for a Bob Dylan recording.

Young people may have the same challenge appreciating the music of prior generations, asking with dismay, "*Was John Denver really that popular back in the day?*" or declaring, "*I don't get this whole Motown thing, 'the sound of young America!'*"

And what is true for music can also be true for our reading. At our best as readers, we both reach back to voices of earlier generations and forward in listening to the voices of young writers today. In my case, I have benefitted greatly by reading the works of people from prior generations such as the late Howard Thurman, an African American writer and chaplain writing in the middle of the twentieth century; Harold Myra, a one-time executive with *Christianity Today*, whose book *Living By God's Surprises* is a touchstone; and Thomas Merton, a Cistercian monk and author of classics such as *The Seven Storey Mountain* and *No Man is an Island.* I've benefitted from reading forward with younger generations of writers and thinkers such as Jen Pollock Michel, Sho Baraka, Justin Whitmel Earley, and Marlena Graves. Each generation brings gifts through their writings, and each has shortcomings. By reading diverse generational voices, we are exposed to wisdom through the ages, and we continue to grow as the years increase.

Loving Our Neighbors By Seeing Them

Helen Lee, author of *The Race Wise Family*, is a person who has consistently helped me see the value of (and remain committed to) reading diverse authors as part of our discipline of reading. She sees this commitment as an expression of loving our neighbors well. Lee says:

> Loving our neighbors is not merely a suggestion but one of the greatest commands that Jesus gave to his disciples and to the church as a whole. And reading can be a wonderful vehicle by which we can grow in our capacity to live out this commandment. As Mary McCampbell writes in *Imagining Our Neighbors as Ourselves: How Art Shapes Empathy*, "Good art challenges us into having eyes that see our neighbors, and many times, these neighbors look, speak, and live very differently than we do. . . . Art that enables us to imagine our neighbors as ourselves continually points back to the greatest Artist."
>
> As we become acquainted with a wide range of authors from backgrounds different than our own, who introduce us to contexts, experiences, and cultures with which we may not be familiar, we grow in our understanding of those unique settings and characters, which then has an impact on our present realities. Our hearts, souls, and minds expand,

> as does our capacity to love. So reading diverse voices is more than just an aspirational ideal; it's a pathway toward Christlikeness.[2]

What a promise—the enlarging of our capacity to love, to see, and to pursue a Christlike pursuit of loving our neighbors as ourselves. Reading can enable us to seek and realize such an aspiration.

~

In the conclusion of her book on the Tulsa Race Massacre, Brandy Colbert writes, "A framed art print hangs in my home that reads ASK MORE QUESTIONS. I've always valued this advice; I see it as a nod to my love of journalism, which I spent four years studying in college. But these words are, first and foremost, a fervent reminder to continue seeking out the truth every day, and to never stop sharing it."[3]

Like Colbert, I studied journalism, and my first job was in that field. Perhaps because of that, I appreciate a steady interrogation of ideas and I value a steady stream of questions. Drawing from diverse voices in our spiritual discipline of reading can help us ask good questions. It can also help us arrive at answers that embody truth, hope, and love, informed by perspectives well beyond our own.

And that is worth the effort.

~

The Importance of Reading Diverse Voices

> I grew up in the 1970s and '80s in a tree-draped Illinois town split by a river. Rockford was a onetime bustling manufacturing hub located 90 miles northwest of Chicago. The Rock River sliced through the city's center, separating east from west, rich from poor, and white from Black and Brown.
>
> I was one of the Black kids chosen to answer the call of public-school desegregation by boarding yellow buses that

carried us across the river to provide white classrooms with a dash of color. Throughout much of my grade school years, I accepted that white people lived on the east side in nice homes with perfectly manicured lawns, while Black and Brown folks lived in rundown houses and overcrowded public-housing apartments where police were seemingly omnipresent. I normalized the inequity and dysfunction.

I had no idea how limited my sense of the world was—that is, until my white public-school education awakened in me a passion for reading that led me to taking notice of literary characters who looked like me, figures like John Henry, Nat Love, and Phillis Wheatley. In middle school, I found myself enamored with the lyrical ponderings of Langston Hughes, Maya Angelou, and Paul Laurence Dunbar. They wrote of crystal stairs, caged birds, and smiling masks. By high school, urgent voices like Lorraine Hansberry, James Baldwin, and Alex Haley were demanding my attention.

Through our mere presence on those school buses, the kids from my neighborhood brought diversity to the predominantly white schools on Rockford's east side. But it was my conversations with the writings of authors of color that taught me that my daily journey to the "white side" of Rockford was not for the purpose of training me to think and see white. Rather, it was an opportunity to learn in a setting that challenged students and teachers alike to see beyond a monocultural perspective. Now, almost fifty years later, as a Black author and reader of Black authors, I recognize that my African American experience is a real and vital part of the human experience. Reading diverse authors broadens and expands our view of the world—and of ourselves.

—**Edward Gilbreath**, author of *Reconciliation Blues* and *Birmingham Revolution*

The Power of Perspective: Reading Diverse Voices

15 Recommended Books

The list of books below reflects insight from a diverse set of authors and on a variety of topics and geographic contexts. Let this list simply be a start (or an encouragement to continue) in your journey of reading perspectives that may be very different from your own, or subject matter that you've yet to engage with.

- *Black Birds in the Sky: The Story and Legacy of the 1921 Tulsa Race Massacre*, by Brandy Colbert
- *Reading Black Books: How African American Literature Can Make Our Faith More Whole and Just*, by Claude Atcho
- *Reading with Patrick: A Teacher, a Student, and a Life-Changing Friendship*, by Michelle Kuo
- *Shoutin' in the Fire: An American Epistle*, by Dante Stewart
- *How Far to the Promised Land*, by Esau McCaulley
- *Caste*, by Isabel Wilkerson
- *Night*, by Elie Wiesel
- *The Race Wise Family*, by Helen Lee and Michelle Ami Reyes
- *One Hundred Saturdays: Stella Levi and the Search for a Lost World*, by Michael Frank
- *The Violence of Love*, by Oscar Romero
- *Meditations of the Heart*, by Howard Thurman
- *The Home That Was Our Country: A Memoir of Syria*, by Alia Malek
- *The Book of Forgiving*, by Desmond Tutu and Mpho Tutu
- *The Cross and the Lynching Tree*, by James Cone
- *Birmingham Revolution: Martin Luther King's Epic Challenge to the Church*, by Edward Gilbreath

"We believe one minute and waver the next. As Screwtape tells his diabolical apprentice about mankind, it is during the lows rather than the highs that a person of faith grows closer to God."

—Carolyn Weber, *Surprised by Oxford*[1]

Chapter Seven
The Power of Reflection: Reading Memoir

It wasn't the most inspiring environment in which to think about writing, creativity, and stories, but it's where we found ourselves on a hot June day on a Midwest Christian college campus as part of a writers conference.

Twenty-five of us were huddled in a cramped, nearly windowless classroom with desks built for people much younger than any of us assembled. We were there to hear the first of three sessions on the subject of memoir writing. I was attending not because I had ever planned to write in the genre but, rather, to understand better what it is that has drawn me to it in recent years. After decades of faithfully reading biographies or autobiographies of major figures in US, world, and church history, my reading memoir is a relatively new category in my reading as a spiritual discipline.

Why?

As the speaker dipped into her subject matter, I was struck by the answers I heard. Memoir, she said, prompts empathy for another person in a way most other nonfiction writing cannot do. They are the *memories* (thus, the genre name) of another person, not simply chronological facts we typically find in biography and autobiography. They begin with some significant event, which could have happened at any point in the author's life, and they make their way backward and forward from that, attempting to make sense of the story of their lives.

Whether or not we ever write a memoir of our own, isn't that what much of our reading and reflecting and, if we are journal keepers, our writing is attempting to do—to help us make sense of our own story, embrace our story, perhaps share our story with another?

"Though there is the existing stereotype that memoirs can be overdramatic and exaggerated, the genre allows its readers to be exposed to new perspectives and gather the wisdom of those who have been through unique experiences. Memoirs have the power to inspire by motivating their readers through descriptions of what the author has had to overcome," Nagham Mashraqi writes in an essay for *The Kudzu Review* titled "Memoirs: An Underrated Genre." "They allow you to completely immerse yourself in a story that isn't your own while still reading a narrative that is realistic, something you can picture someone else going through because it's the genuine memories of someone's life."[2]

Though I had occasionally read memoirs in the past, I tended to prefer biographies or autobiographies, genres which were more chronologically structured and offered primarily facts. That was in keeping with reading that was more interested in intellectual propositions, arguments, and defenses of the Christian faith and ideas. However, a memoir rooted in a Canadian woman's story of a short time period in Oxford, England, changed that posture and led me to be a regular reader of memoir.

An Oxford Surprise

We do well to have a Mr. Holland in our lives—someone who, like the Richard Dreyfus character in the 1996 film *Mr. Holland's Opus*, teaches us not merely how to get the grade but how to think. Not merely how to earn a diploma but how to *live*.

Several Mr. Holland figures made their way in and out of author Carolyn Weber's memoir *Surprised by Oxford*, drawing me into the story of a person I'd never heard of, into a book that I had not known until a bookseller friend said, *"Jeff, you must read this book!"* To this day I'm not sure what prompted him to recommend it, but I'm glad he did.

The first and arguably most enduring Mr. Holland figure to enter Weber's story is Dr. Deveaux, a professor of seventeenth-century poetry during the then-Carolyn Drake's undergraduate years at a school in her native Canada.

Drake was reared by a mother with very loose, cultural ties to the church and a mostly absent, unreliable father. She emerged agnostic with a strong sense that she knew who her master was: She was her own.

Deveaux, by contrast, was an evangelical, though in the book Weber acknowledges that she would have had no understanding of that label at the time she studied under his tutelage.

Responding to Miss Drake's assigned reading of John Donne's Sonnet XIV and her argument for the poem's "classic subversion by the dominant patriarchy . . . of the threat posed by maternal power, or the feminine *spiritus*,"[3] Deveaux challenged her reading, insisting that she didn't get the point; that she had not untied a subtle and very important knot in Donne's message.

"The truth is in the paradox, Miss Drake," Weber writes in recounting Professor Deveaux's retort. "Anything not done in submission to God, anything not done to the glory of God, is doomed to failure, frailty, and futility. This is the unholy trinity we humans fear most. And we should, for we entertain it all the time at the pain and expense of not knowing the real one."[4]

Deveaux's comeback did not stop there. In direct language that reminded me of many a professor I've encountered, Deveaux continued: "The rest is all bullshit, Miss Drake. It's as simple as that. And your purpose here in life is to discern the real thing from the bullshit, and then to choose the non-bullshit."[5]

Shortly thereafter, Carolyn Drake matriculated to Oriel College at Oxford University, where, leaving a fellow agnostic fiancé back in

Canada, she began work toward her Master of Philosophy degree, focusing on writers such as Coleridge, Goethe, Blake, Keats, Shelley, Wordsworth, and Byron. Through a series of encounters with other Mr. Hollands and just as many anti-Hollands, she cut through the B.S. and found her purpose, just as Deveaux challenged her to do.

That journey is recounted in *Surprised by Oxford*, a memoir of Weber's first year there, which is also the story of her conversion. Her narrative is structured around the terms of the school's academic year, embedded in the Christian liturgical calendar: Michaelmas, Hilary, and Trinity, with interludes around Christmastide and Eastertide. Weber's debt to C. S. Lewis's *Surprised by Joy* is acknowledged in her book's title, but *Surprised by Oxford* is different in many respects from Lewis's memoir, with a significantly more truncated timeframe, much faster pacing, and more troubled childhood roots that set up the book's narrative and tension. It also has hints of Francis Thompson's *The Hound of Heaven*, with God seemingly pursuing Weber at every turn, not only through some of her professors but also via a madcap group of friends (believers and skeptics alike) who frequent the famous Oxford pub The Eagle and Child for conversations about the meaning of life—and the music of U2.

Surprised by Oxford is, in short, a moving portrait of one woman's intellectual and spiritual conversion. It is a story for all of us who find ourselves uttering on occasion, with the father of the ill son in the Gospel of Mark, "Lord, I do believe; help me overcome my unbelief!"—a prayer that proved to be a centerpiece in Weber's conversion.

"That man's desperate plea for the overcoming of his unbelief echoed deep within me, leaving nowhere to hide," Weber writes. "God had called out even this very last façade, this trump card of an excuse, this very final resting place of despair. And it appeared that for us particularly hard nuts to crack the only answer is prayer."[6]

And so she prayed. And she believed.

Ultimately, Weber was baptized in the River Thames on Trinity Sunday of Trinity Term, just after a service at St. Ebbe's Church. At the end of her baptismal day, she sat on an old bench by the river and opened a gift from one of her madcap friends, Hannah. On the underside of the gift box were the words from Milton's *Paradise Lost* in Hannah's handwriting. They read:

> *And fast by hanging in a golden chain*
> *This pendent world, in bigness as a star*
> *Of smallest magnitude close by the moon*[7]

Weber pulled out a beautiful piece of sea glass attached to a fine, silver chain. "I drew it out carefully, admiring how the sea jewel's brilliant blues and greens shimmered in suspension against the red and orange flame," Weber writes with elegance and detail.

> "My breath caught at its seeming fragility, at its bright and bold beauty.
> "How can we be so small, and so significant?
> "Yes.
> "Boxes and boxes of paradoxes! Open them all up, and therein glistens the gift of truth."[8]

Professor Deveaux did not live to hear a firsthand account of Weber's surprise in Oxford. But I suspect he would have been delighted by her acceptance of the gift of triune truth, in the midst of its paradoxes.

An Object Lesson

Surprised by Oxford became something of an object lesson for me, demonstrating the power of a memoir that, in the words of a writer friend named Karen Stiller, ponders rather than preaches, explores rather than explains. Many other touchstone memoirs have followed, including Jeannette Walls's *The Glass Castle*, the late Congressman John Lewis's *Walking with the Wind*, civil rights leader Andrew Young's *A Way Out of No Way*, Doris Kearns Goodwin's *An Unfinished Love*

Story, Anna Gazmarian's *Devout: A Memoir of Doubt*, J. Dana Trent's *Between Two Trailers*, and Beth Moore's *All My Knotted-Up Life*. What all of them (and many others) have in common is an ability to draw the reader into the story of their lives and to provoke introspection about their own.

Psychologists speak of the act of memoir writing as a transformative experience, moving our feelings from a subterranean space onto a page and, in doing so, allowing us to work through challenges or celebrate stories of things we have overcome in our lives. It's one of the values of journaling, I believe, even if we never intend to share what lands on paper with another person.

Diana Raab has written in *Psychology Today*, "We transform when we write about our lived experiences because writing helps us make sense of them and also reminds us of the lessons we've learned along the way. Sometimes when looking back at a life event, it's easier to see it in the grand, universal spectrum of life rather than as an isolated experience."[9]

Might reading memoir do the same? I tend to think it just might.

A Surprising Yet Familiar Story

On a spring day not long ago, a package arrived on my doorstep containing a copy of a new book release from a writer I'd never encountered, though she had written several previous works. The title was intriguing: *Between Two Trailers: A Memoir*, and a foreword by Barbara Brown Taylor, a writer I respect highly, was another prompt to pick it up and read.

The book was sent by a former colleague whose judgment I trust, and so I dipped into J. Dana Trent's memoir the same evening, even though I had several other books in the ever-expanding reading cue.

Within the first 50 pages of *Between Two Trailers*, I was brought to tears by Trent's prose, by her story, by its proximity to my own—and, most significantly, by the grace and forgiveness she extended to her troubled parents, and the dignity she expressed for the slightly down-on-their-luck towns in the so-called fly-over portion of the American Midwest that both Trent and I had once called home. The early portions of the book were set in two small western Indiana towns that the author and I shared in common, the places we both lived and went to school in during our childhoods, separated by just a few city blocks but more than 20 years. As I approached the halfway point of the book, when Trent's story shifts from Indiana to North Carolina, I commented to my wife, "If you read just the first half of this book, I think you might understand me and my story even better than you already do." And we have been married for more than four decades.

Reading Trent's memoir was a profound experience, not unlike reading *Surprised by Oxford* 15 years earlier. Memoirs have the power to do that. To help us understand the stories of our own lives, even as we are reading about the unique story of the author.

Listening to Our Lives

The memoirist who has done her or his work well, like J. Dana Trent and Carolyn Weber, has first listened to their lives well—to the pain, the joy, the grace, the forgiveness, the hope present in them. And with that gift in hand, they are ready to share it with us, their readers. As Barbara Brown Taylor wrote in the foreword to *Between Two Trailers*, Trent shared her memories not only for herself but also for us, "to remind us that there is more at work in all of our stories than any of us knows. Wounds and blessings come in matched pairs, at least if we're willing to wrestle them to the ground."[10]

This is the very thing that Frederick Buechner asked of his readers in his memoir of faith and vocation titled *Now and Then*. "Listen to your life. See it for the fathomless mystery that it is," Frederick Buechner wrote. "In the boredom and pain of it no less than in the excitement and gladness: touch, taste, smell your way to the holy and hidden heart of it because in the last analysis all moments are key moments, and life itself is grace."[11]

The attention we give to memoir as part of our spiritual discipline of reading can open up insights not only on the stories of others, but on our own sacred story, as well. Thanks be to God for the "wounds and blessings" that "come in matched pairs" in the story of all of our lives.

~

The Power of Reflection: Memoirs and More

> I had an epiphany in 1951 shortly after I visited the Public Library in Compton, California. I had never seen such a thing in all my nine years. Mrs. Custer, my fourth-grade teacher, had taken my class on a field trip of sorts, to introduce us to the wonders of a place where we could borrow and take home any book we wanted from that sacred place. Any book?! At the time I was passionately interested in spaceships and armor: interplanetary travel and aliens, and anyone I ever heard once wore armor—Romans and medieval knights. The library was full of books like that. I checked out a bunch. Later I discovered there were books about other things. So one day came the epiphany: I could read everything there was to read in that place, and know everything there was to know! And I set out to do so. I'm 82 years old as I write this, 73 years after my vision. Of course I'm nowhere near the grand vision I had as a nine-year-old. And I've learned that Francis Bacon was right: "Some books should be tasted, some devoured, but only a few should be chewed and digested thoroughly." But I also agree with Robert Browning: "Ah, but a man's reach should exceed his grasp or what's a heaven for?"
>
> —**Ben Patterson,** author of *The Grand Essentials* and *When God Showed Up: A Memoir*

The Power of Reflection: Reading Memoir

15 Recommended Memoirs

Below is a list of seminal books in the memoir genre. Some are written from a perspective of Christian faith, one from a Jewish point of view. All of them have a poignant story to tell.

- *Telling Secrets*, by Frederick Buechner
- *Between Two Trailers*, by J. Dana Trent
- *I Know Why the Caged Bird Sings*, by Maya Angelou
- *Surprised by Joy*, by C. S. Lewis
- *Where the Light Fell*, by Philip Yancey
- *You Could Make This Place Beautiful*, by Maggie Smith
- *No Cure for Being Human (And Other Truths I Needed to Hear)*, by Kate Bowler
- *Walking with the Wind*, by John Lewis
- *The Shaping of a Life: A Spiritual Landscape*, by Phyllis Tickle
- *Surprised by Oxford*, by Carolyn Weber
- *All Rivers Run to the Sea*, by Elie Wiesel
- *All Is Grace*, by Brennan Manning
- *The Glass Castle*, by Jeannette Walls
- *All My Knotted-Up Life*, by Beth Moore
- *The Sacred Journey*, by Frederick Buechner

Part Three
Reading Through Seasons of Life and Faith

"Good reading, therefore, though it is not essentially an affectional or moral or intellectual activity, has something in common with all three. In love we escape from our self into one other."

—C. S. Lewis, *An Experiment in Criticism*[1]

Chapter Eight: Reading in Seasons of Family Life

It's interesting the things we hold onto over the course of a lifetime when so much we accumulate is simply handed down to the next generations, taken in cardboard boxes to a nearby thrift store, or set out with bags destined for a landfill.

Some things we cherish over time for obvious reasons: We are reminded of a loved one who is no longer with us, or a pivotal time in our life. We're reminded of a place that felt deeply like home, or a friend who was sustaining to us in a crucial moment.

At other times we hold onto something for reasons that evade understanding.

Aside from photographs my mother has handed down in a keepsake journal *Reflections From a Mother's Heart* that she prepared for me a number of years ago, the oldest possession I carry with me from childhood is a book. I find that curious, since I was not an avid reader as a young person. But something about this book—given as a gift—has prompted me to keep it tucked away in my library for more than five decades. Perhaps it's the connection it has to that season of my family's life more than fifty years ago, a season of change and dislocation.

I suspect there were other books I owned, read, and loved as a child prior to this one, but if so I have no recollection of them. The relic I've kept with me is an oversized book that was labeled as volume six in the Educator Classic Library and published by Classic Press in Santa Rosa, California. The series, containing 12 books in all, was comprised of what the editors at the time deemed classics of Western literature suitable for elementary-aged children: *Pinocchio*, *The Merry Adventures of Robin Hood*, *Swiss Family Robinson*, *20,000 Leagues Under the Sea*, *The Jungle Book*, *Casebook of Sherlock Holmes*, and *The Call of the Wild* were among the other entries in the set, abridged and illustrated with pencil drawings that were likely lavish for the time (but woefully out of date today).

Volume six was *The Virginian* by Owen Wister, a writer who was a Harvard University classmate and friend of future US President Theodore Roosevelt and who was called "the father of Western fiction."

The original book, serialized by *Harper's Magazine*, was said to have spawned the growth of cowboy television shows for years after its release, including *Bonanza*, *Ponderosa*, *The Big Valley*, *Gunsmoke*, *The Rifleman*, and, of course, *The Virginian*. And though I wasn't reading a lot of books in the 1960s, I *was* faithfully watching those vintage Westerns!

The words written inside the front cover of my aged, yellowed copy of *The Virginian* are "Merry Christmas 1970, from Aunt Micki and the Cousins." I was nine years old, and my family had moved that year to the other side of the country. Our aunt gave my older brother a volume from J. R. R. Tolkien's *Lord of the Rings* trilogy, while my younger brother received one of the seven entries in C. S. Lewis's *Chronicles of Narnia* set that same day.

They received books about Middle Earth and an enchanting wardrobe. I received the cowboy story, and I loved it. Books were one of the ways my aunt, whom all three of us boys dearly loved and who we would later live with for a short time during another family transition, maintained a sense of connection with us.

Today, after spending an adult lifetime working in the world of books, I see the ways in which reading throughout the seasons of our life equips us, motivates us, and guides us in navigating challenges, wrestling with questions, and seizing opportunities before us. I also see the ways in which reading knits generations together, passing along values and perspectives and discovering new ways of looking at the world. And I see the ways in which reading helps us move through the inevitable seasons of change and loss in our family life, including caring for grandchildren or being a part of eldercare as our parents' health declines.

There is something almost mysterious about the ways in which books bind individuals and families together. Perhaps it's as C. S. Lewis suggests, that reading allows us to escape from ourselves, even if for just a short while, into one another.

Reading in Seasons with Children

In the early 1980s, two years prior to the birth of our first child, my wife and I left jobs working for small-town daily newspapers and began operating our bookstore. Books became a source not only of income for our young family but also a centerpiece of our parenting and family life as we expanded from two to four people with the arrival of a son and, two years later, a daughter. Each night, we would read stories to our children, gradually moving from infant board books to Little Golden Books like *The Poky Little Puppy* and *Tootle*, from *The Velveteen Rabbit* to *Goodnight Moon* and the retelling of biblical parables in the Adam Raccoon series, from the Gospel metaphor of *The Tale of Three Trees* to George Macdonald's *Sir Gibbie*, from teach-yourself-the-French-language books to J. R. R. Tolkien's *The Hobbit* and the *Lord of the Rings* trilogy.

Trips to our town's public library became ritualistic events, and we would bring stacks of books home and make our way through them both together and on our own, discovering new writers and illustrators whom our children responded to.

"I remember those trips to the library and being so excited to choose a new book," my daughter, now 37 and a teacher of Italian in a public high school, recently wrote to me. "I remember always having bedtime reading and as I got older, staying up late with my nightlight to finish a good book. I also remember long trips in a car or on a plane long before devices were common and reading so much to pass the time."

Even as a young girl, she studied languages through the reading of books, eventually taking a trip to France when she was in elementary school with a high school group led by the mother of one of her friends. One can easily see how her reading shaped her educational journey when later she studied in Florence, Italy, and now impacts her vocational work as an Italian language teacher taking students on immersive learning experiences in Italy.

Our son, two years older and now working in finance on the Eastern Seaboard of the US, acknowledged in a recent conversation that he didn't like to sit still as a child or even in adolescence. He was always on the move. As a result, he wasn't really an avid reader then, though he would participate in times of family reading. But today, he's among the most voracious readers that I encounter, never without a book with him on the train he takes to and from his Pennsylvania home into New York City for work. He consistently recommends books to my wife and me—works he's read and been impacted by—and often sends copies of those books to us for birthdays or Christmas gifts. He credits the seeds sown in his childhood for the reader he has become today. "And it's now my turn to plant in my four kids the exposure, appreciation, and discipline of reading—on and on, from one generation to the next," he says.

And he's doing that.

Writing well before the advent of digital tablets, phones, and video streaming services, when sitting in front of a television set was a primary form of entertainment for children, author Terry Glaspey wrote, "One of the greatest gifts we can give to our children is to introduce them to the joys of reading. From the earliest ages, children love to be read to. Books they cannot read for themselves may be thoroughly enjoyed when you read aloud to them. And this enjoyment may continue longer than you'd think."[2]

Today, we regularly read aloud to grandchildren who live nearby (and occasionally via FaceTime to four who live some distance away), and there are touchstone books like *Castaway Cats*, a book about cooperation and community, that all six of them can virtually read by heart. They take turns reading pages, and know just where to be ready to exclaim, "I think we're in a jam!" as that lively page rolls around. Of late, the out-of-town grandchildren proactively ask to FaceTime so they can read their new discoveries to us. It's wonderful to see language come alive through their distinctive voices, and to sense the pride they feel as they read ever more challenging books aloud to us.

Even if we do not have children or grandchildren of our own, chances are that most of us are connected to young people in some way through extended family, church communities, or friendships. Our modeling the value of reading plants the seeds, as our son has told us, that may not bear fruit for a while. But if and when they do, the world of wonders that opens up within their lives will be worth all of the work we have done to scatter seeds in their lives.

"Fortunately, there is no shortage of stories of another sort: books that challenge, thrill, and excite, and awaken young readers to the potential drama of life, especially to the drama of a life lived in obedience to the highest ideals. Like true friends, they encourage us to be our best selves," write William Kilpatrick, Gregory Wolfe, and Suzanne Wolfe in *Books That Build Character.*[3]

Although our family has many touchstone books we have shared with one another, one series stands out above all others, and they teach not only character but also parables modeled on stories from the Bible. They are books that sought to inspire us to live "in obedience to the highest ideals."

In 1987, Glen Keane released the first of a series of parables for children whose protagonist was a lively, mischievous raccoon named Adam. The illustrations immediately captivated me when I saw the first volume, *Adam Raccoon at Forever Falls*, arrive in our store. And with good reason. Not only was Glen Keane an animation director at Walt Disney Pictures, but also his father, Bill, was the creator and animator of the enduring comic strip *Family Circus*, which was launched in 1960 and continues to run today under the direction of his youngest son, Jeff. *Family Circus* was a strip I never missed reading in the Sunday newspaper that would land on my family's porch as I was growing up, and the illustrations in the Adam Raccoon series evoked the joy and wonder I always found in that syndicated comic.

The Adam Raccoon series would eventually expand to eight volumes, each with a thematic focus of importance for children and adults alike: love, forgiveness, faithfulness, discipleship, salvation, and more. Those books became such markers of our family's reading life together that all of our grandchildren eventually received a set and read them with such interest that they could virtually recite each page from memory even before they could read. Like the parables of Christ in the New Testament Gospels, these books were memorable, accessible, and compelling. The wallpaper on the iPad I carry with me on long business trips has a picture of grandson Jack and granddaughter Anna reading *Adam Raccoon and the Circus Master* (on the parable of the lost son).

That series of books and many other individual works not only have been entertaining and instructional, but also they have built memories and connecting tissues across the generations and seasons of our family life.

Seasons of Letting Go

Reading is important not only in seasons with young children but also as they grow and transition into lives and families of their own, largely independent of our guidance as parents.

After Cindy and I dropped our son off for his first year of undergraduate studies at a university in central Pennsylvania, I quickly realized that I was not prepared for the impact of his absence in our home or on me as his father. Even as we drove the ten hours west after leaving him on campus for the first time, I was filled with questions: How do we maintain a connection at a distance? What does it mean to be the parent of a young adult? How do I let go of what I have known with him and re-fashion something new? What will he need?

Two years later we made another trip even further east, dropping our daughter off at a university in the heart of New York City. Although we had some experience with this type of change by then, similar questions returned and in some ways were heightened now that our home was absent both children who brought such vitality, energy, and, yes, at times, noise, into the home.

Talking to friends who were just a few years ahead of me in this journey of letting go was one path of both solace and instruction, but reading was another path. I found in the pages of books immense wisdom about our seasons as human persons, as roles were redefined and we experienced both the losses and the new life amid those changes. This season drove me into deeper reading in spiritual formation, with books such as Richard Rohr's *Falling Upward: A Spirituality for the Two Halves of Life*, offering wisdom for what was rapidly becoming my second half in those days of letting go.

Perhaps you have not had the experience of letting go of children, but you undoubtedly have had similar seasons of letting go—jobs, homes, parents, or other things. The value of reading as a spiritual discipline in seasons of letting go applies to those transitions, as well.

Seasons of Caring for Aging Parents

If reading plays a role in the seasons of our family life as we parent children and as we let go or face other transitions, I am finding that it also has an unexpected but vital role as we step into caring for aging parents, those who may have read with and to us when we were children long ago. Those who may need us to read to them, or on their behalf today.

As I write these pages, I am in a season of family life that most of us experience at some point. As our parents age and face mental or physical health challenges, we step into new roles and care for them as best we can, sometimes (as in my case) at a considerable geographic distance. In this season, I've been accompanied by books written specifically to help me understand vexing challenges such as dementia, brain neuroscience, and other health issues. They are also tutoring me in how to honor and extend dignity to aging parents, attending to physical, social, emotional, and spiritual needs. These resources also commonly remind readers of the caregiver's limitations and needs, as well.

Reading in this season of my life has reminded me of the season 40 years ago, when I looked to books to understand what it meant to be a good father, how to parent well, and what to do when I was at my wits' end. It has felt like a return to those almost basic, foundational questions: How do I care well? What does it mean to be a good son (or brother, or sister) in this time? How do I convey dignity? How do I use this time we have remaining well?

Thankfully, others have gone before me and have written about it. The guidance is there, both in Scripture and in books.

Reading in Seasons of Family Life

I've had coffee with talented physicians, enjoyed a sunrise with discerning psychologists, garnered wisdom from secluded monks. I have met only a few of them, but each of them has left a mark on me. Their writings challenge, mentor and comfort me. They willingly meet me in the quiet of the morning at my dining room table. When I create space, they will always meet me there.

These authors have mentored me in how to navigate the changes that come to every family. They offered me new tools and skills my parents never had. Through reading their books, I learned how to help my children wrestle with tough questions rather than giving them the answer. I learned how my spouse and I could grow closer instead of drifting apart as we watched so many couples do. I learned how best to help my father as my mother's dementia took her from us and then took her life.

When I open their books and open my heart, an author's words shape me into a better husband, better father and better grandfather one lesson, one skill, one page at a time.

—Greg Bowman, pastor and co-author of *Leading Life-Changing Small Groups*

Reading in Seasons of Family Life

15 Recommended Works

Below is a list of books primarily for reading with children. However, I have also included recommendations of other resources that touch on themes of the chapter including cultivating rhythms in a family life (with children, grandchildren, or others), and processing seasons of letting go.

- *The Boy, the Mole, the Fox and the Horse*, written and illustrated by Charlie Mackesy
- *Castaway Cats*, by Lisa Wheeler with art by Ponder Goembel
- *The Tale of Three Trees: A Traditional Folktale*, by Angela Elwell Hunt
- *The Adam Raccoon series* (eight volumes), written and illustrated by Glen Keane
- *The Tree of Here*, by Chaim Potok
- *Thoughtfull: Discovering the Unique Gifts in Each of Us*, by Dorena Williamson
- *The Book of Virtues*, edited by William J. Bennett
- *The Chronicles of Narnia*, by C. S. Lewis
- *The Lord of the Rings Trilogy*, by J. R. R. Tolkien
- *Sir Gibbie*, by George MacDonald
- *God's Beloved Community*, by Michelle Sanchez, illustrated by Camila Carrossine
- *Reading Magic: Why Reading Aloud to Our Children Will Change Their Lives Forever*, by Mem Fox
- *Habits of the Household: Practicing the Story of God in Everyday Family Rhythms*, by Justin Whitmel Earley
- *Falling Upward*, by Richard Rohr
- *Finding Grace in the Face of Dementia*, by John Dunlop, MD

"Being alive means suffering loss. Sometimes the loss is predictable, and even reversible. It occurs at regular intervals, like the seasons. . . . But there is a different kind of loss that inevitably occurs in all of our lives, though less frequently and certainly less predictably. This kind of loss has more devastating results, and it is irreversible."[1]

—Jerry Sittser, *A Grace Disguised*

Chapter Nine
Reading in Seasons of Grief and Loss

On a mid-July evening in 2019, I packed a bag for a week-long vacation with my wife, our two adult children, and their families in southwest Florida. Tucked inside my carry-on was a book that may have struck my fellow Southwest Airlines passengers as odd—*Flight 232: A Story of Disaster and Survival* by Laurence Gonzales, published on the twenty-fifth anniversary of a United Airlines crash at Sioux City, Iowa's Gateway Airport on July 19, 1989.

"Why read a book like *that* on a flight?" I imagined my seatmate asking. A fair question.

Although my occupation for more than four decades has required me to travel extensively, I have for years harbored more than a casual fear of flight, especially on take-offs and landings. I've developed a number of coping mechanisms and spiritual practices to deal with the fear, including one that may be unusual: reading about commercial aviation tragedies such as what happened on United flight 232 as it made its way from Denver's Stapleton International Airport to O'Hare International in Chicago. Reading about the rare occasions when something *does* go terribly wrong in flight has brought about an odd sense of reassurance about the unlikelihood of it ever happening to me.

Still, why not pack a Nicholas Sparks novel instead as I headed to the beach? Another good question.

After buckling into my seat on the Boeing 737-700 and listening to the humorous safety overview from chatty Southwest Airlines flight attendants, I opened *Flight 232* and began reading. The first words I encountered were the name of a person: Gregory S. Clapper. Clapper served as the chaplain for the 185th Tactical Fighter Group of the Iowa National Guard, which was stationed at the Sioux City airport. On that July day in 1989, Clapper was traveling to a nearby cinema with his wife, Jody, and their two young daughters, Laura and Jenna, not far from the airport to see the original version of the Walt Disney picture *Peter Pan*, which was then in rerelease with much fanfare.

"As the family crossed the hot paving toward the theater at the Southern Hills Mall, a sudden roaring whine turned Clapper's gaze skyward. Silhouetted against a bright sky, the dark form of a jumbo jet, low and tremendous, surged over the bluffs, its engines moaning in an odd uneven fashion," Gonzales writes. Clapper and his family stood in the parking lot for just a few seconds when "a reef of black smoke rose and coiled from behind the industrial buildings, and a low, almost imperceptible, rumbling vibration shook the pavement. Clapper felt his face go clammy."[2]

Engine failure led to a loss of hydraulics and a destabilization of the aircraft that the flight crew could not overcome. The United DC-10 aircraft had crashed as it attempted to make an emergency landing at Gateway Airport, sending plumes of smoke into the air above the runway and adjacent corn fields. Images broadcast that night would lead one to believe no one could survive what happened. Remarkably, 183 of those on board survived, despite the fact that the jet cartwheeled down the runway, breaking into multiple pieces as it did so.

Clapper's wife took their two daughters into the cinema, while he rushed to the airport—part of the way by car, and part on foot when he reached emergency barricades—to do what any person in his role of chaplain would do: offer consolation, prayers, and presence to the wounded and dying.

Reading Foreshadowing a Need

I finished *Flight 232* within 24 hours of arriving at the vacation site in Florida, and ordered a copy of Clapper's *When the World Breaks Your Heart* for delivery by the time I returned home seven days later.

Little did I know how much I would need his work of consolation on the printed page.

In the intervening days while we were still vacationing on the Gulf Coast, my wife received a cancer diagnosis via a phone call from her primary care physician to the townhome where we were staying with our family. Tests taken the week prior to our departure, out of, doctors had said, "an abundance of caution," had come back with unexpected news. A malignancy. We were told to set up an appointment with an oncologist immediately after we returned home three days later to understand the course of treatment, and the next steps we should take. Our lives were turned upside down. Our hearts were broken.

Cindy and I quietly walked to a nearby pub we have long loved called The Mucky Duck and, with glasses of iced tea in hand, we gazed out on the rhythmic sights and sounds of the Gulf of Mexico and began to ponder what it all meant, and what we had to do.

Gregory Clapper's book was on our doorstep when we returned home, and I read it that night and re-read it multiple times in the months to follow. Although he was specifically addressing how people cope with *tragedy*, in its pages I found deep companionship in that season of grief and intense spiritual and medical questioning. His written counsel regarding mystery, tears, humility, gentleness, hope, and the presence of God merged to console as questions of life and death came into sharp focus for us. Although the calendar said it was August, we had entered a wintry season that would call for courage and hope. Clapper's book nurtured both in my own spirit.

The Ministry of Words

Certain seasons of our lives beg for the ministry of words on a printed page more urgently than others. They are "wintry" seasons of our hearts during which we are called to navigate losses both predictable and unpredictable; to process grief related to unwelcome losses or change that can be reversible or, more chillingly, irreversible.

They are seasons of deep grief or profound loss, which we will all face at one time or another. They are a part of the human experience. Differences in that experience are a matter of degrees rather than whether or not it will happen. Where do we go in such seasons? Certainly, we may turn to a spouse, partner, or trusted friend. We may seek the listening ear of a spiritual director or a therapist. The liturgies of the church handed down through centuries can be sources of healing and hope in such times.

But there are also books: the practice of reading, reflecting, and responding in these seasons.

Many of the books with the most enduring impact on my life have been either preparation for or companions in these wintry seasons, in periods of walking through darkness of grief and loss. Times of grief and loss prompt questions in one's soul, and the companionable books reassure us readers that we are not alone in our questions, fears, and anxieties. We are reminded that others have gone before us, and we soak in their wisdom. We see in the pages before us their example of faithfulness. The writings have also been touchstones in times of a sense of seeming spiritual abandonment when the question "Where are you, God?" is on the tips of our tongues. They have provided solace when unexpected and serious health issues have arisen in a loved one's life, as they did on that July morning in Florida, or in our own.

Books like Gregory Clapper's *When the World Breaks Your Heart.*

As I reflect back on more than 40 years of reading in such seasons, I find on my shelves books with descriptive titles such as *Disappointment with God, Where is God When It Hurts?, A Grace Disguised, Lament for a Son, Good Grief, Grieving a Suicide, Learning to Walk in the Dark, Everything Happens for a Reason (And Other Lies I've Loved), A Cry of Absence*, and *Dark Clouds Deep Mercy*. In each case, I am reminded of how they stepped into a void where only a few safe and trusted people could walk with me. This type of reading has served as something like steppingstones back into light, back to hope, faith, joy as I emerged from those wintry seasons. Rather than escaping the questions and the grief by other means (some healthy, some not), reading in seasons of this type of anguish has been a consistent source of processing, leading to change and transformation.

Through the ages, writers have wrestled with grief and loss, and their stories have pointed the way through the questions that surface with poignancy and power. C. S. Lewis did so as he wrote under the pseudonym N. W. Clerk and put his grief about the illness and eventual death of his wife Helen Joy Davidman (referred to in the book only as "H") down on paper with words that resonate more than six decades later through *A Grief Observed*, words that sound nothing like the confident and convicting ones first shared over the BBC airwaves in what became *Mere Christianity*. Lewis, known for works of apologetics and theological reflection in books like that one and *The Problem of Pain* and fictional works including *The Chronicles of Narnia* and *Till We Have Faces*, poured his grief onto the printed page and in doing so, offered a source of companionship in our own times of grief and questioning God's presence (or absence) in our lives. Reading it recently with fresh eyes, I came away understanding anew why Lewis chose to use N. W. Clerk rather than his own name on the book's cover when it was originally published, because of the uncharacteristic level of vulnerability in its pages.

The book is arguably more popular today than when it released in 1960. In one of the memorable passages from *A Grief Observed*, Lewis writes of God:

> But go to Him when your need is desperate, when all other help is vain, and what do you find? A door slammed in your face, and a sound of bolting and double bolting on the inside. And after that, silence.[3]

Writing of the impact of *A Grief Observed* in a foreword to a later edition of the book, author Madeleine L'Engle wrote, "I am grateful to Lewis for having the courage to yell, to doubt, to kick at God with angry violence. This is a part of healthy grief not often encouraged. It is helpful indeed that C.S. Lewis who has been such a successful apologist for Christianity should have the courage to admit doubt about what he has so superbly proclaimed. It gives us permission to admit our own doubts, our own angers and anguishes, and to know that they are part of the soul's growth."[4]

Reading in seasons of grief and loss can, indeed, be a part of the soul's growth. I've seen that in my own life and the lives of others who are a part of my community of faith, my circle of friends.

And in the life of my mother.

The Call You Never Want to Receive

It was mid-afternoon when a phone call came into the bookstore I operated with my wife, Cindy, and the unexpected caller was my family's longtime physician. He was the same person I saw for vaccinations and checkups as a child and adolescent, but he'd never called *me* before. His message was short and to the point. I needed to get to the hospital as soon as possible. The call was about my mother, a woman in her mid-40s at the time.

We traveled an hour north to the hospital where she had been hospitalized for what turned out to be an advanced stage of cancer, with a bleak prognosis. The doctor who called suggested she likely had four months to live and told us that "your family should ensure her affairs are in order."

In the weeks that followed, my mother—always a reader, in my memory, though of novelists whose works have long been forgotten—asked us to bring her books that would offer hope in the midst of what seemed like a hopeless situation. She wanted to read books that would shed light in the darkness she was feeling. She wanted to talk about heaven, a topic I couldn't recall ever having a conversation with her about before. Scouring the shelves of our bookstore for titles that had offered such light to either us or our customers, we pulled a few and took them with us on our next trip. The only books I remember specifically were Max Lucado's *No Wonder They Call Him the Savior* and its follow-up, *God Came Near*, books of an inspirational nature that I believed might encourage her and offer a sense that God would, indeed, come very near to her in that time of need.

More than four decades later, she is still living. For years prior to a recent move to a new city, she worshipped at and served in volunteer capacities at a United Methodist church, counting up weekly tithes and offerings and assisting in a food pantry. She continues to read and is as likely as anyone I know to be the one to pass along books of hope and comfort to others in *their* times of loss. Through words on a printed page, through friendships, through family, and through the mystery of the incarnation, God did come near—Immanuel, the Christ, her hope of glory. I recognize that her story of survival is not the way such painful journeys often turn out.

Grief. Hope. Held in our hands and hearts, simultaneously.

In a wise post to a site called Grateful Living, the Bloomington, Indiana-based folk musician Carrie Newcomer captured the reality of grief and hope being held together in tension when she wrote, "Part of our collective story is how to meaningfully hold grief and hope, acknowledging what cannot be changed and still envisioning all that can."[5]

Preparing for Wintry Seasons

Reading in our wintry seasons is well served, I believe, by preparing ourselves in our summer seasons—when grief and loss are not acute. It's helped by reading the accounts of others who have gone before us in their own journeys of grief and loss and who have shown us a way through their reflections, their processing, their wisdom. There is an effect of preparing for what is inevitably to come and being ready to respond with courage and hope.

When the pandemic descended on the world in the late winter of 2020, reading and praying the Book of Psalms daily through a book titled *In the Lord I Take Refuge* was among the spiritual practices that sustained me as each day's news brought more sobering data, more conflicting stories, and more division. A book that pairs each of the 150 Psalms of Scripture with a devotional reflection by Dane Ortlund, *In the Lord I Take Refuge* was literally a book in which I took refuge and derived hope for the road ahead. I was prepared for that, however, through prior devotional readings of the Psalms, where I encountered every emotion I was experiencing, every lament I felt, and authentic pleas to God for refuge, for light.

In a similar way, reading Marilyn McEntyre's *A Long Letting Go*, which offers meditations on facing our fears as we lose a loved one, before we face the need to actually let go, nurtures an understanding and a preparation for what all of us will inevitably face. And in doing so, we have prayers, vigils, and liturgies at our sides when our work of caregiving is required.

Engaging with books like Kate Bowler's memoirs *Everything Happens for a Reason (And Other Lies I've Loved)* and *No Cure for Being Human (And Other Truths I Need to Hear)*, which detail her journey with cancer, are instructive for those of us who long to walk faithfully even if our own story is dramatically different from the one she poignantly tells.

Such understanding and preparation are why I ordered Gregory Clapper's book in a summer season of my own life, not knowing how quickly it would turn to winter.

In the closing pages of Gregory Clapper's book *When the World Breaks Your Heart*, he wrote reassuring words that I have returned to time and time again in wintry seasons. May they anchor you in your own seasons of grief and loss, as well.

> Because God chose to live in time, then so can we—so *must* we. With all of its contingencies, failures, and shortcomings, time is where God calls us to live. God calls us to enter into

> this moving stream of life where emotions live. Time is the home of emotions, and emotions are the home where *we* live. Time and the human heart are the arenas of God's presence.[6]

Books, like the one Clapper chose to write out of his experiences in Iowa on a July day in 1989, are also arenas of God's presence and God's provision. Thanks be to God.

~

On Reading in Seasons of Grief and Loss

> There is nothing in life heavier to carry than a grieving heart—be it the loss of a loved one, the loss of a marriage, the loss of hair to chemotherapy or the loss of a dream unrealized. But like a trusted friend who abides with us and never forsakes us when the sorrows of life hit home, books—and the stories they bear—gift us similarly, holding space for our suffering, providing witness to our pain, and illumining paths toward healing.
>
> Through my own experiences with grief and loss, I have found the discipline of reading not only to be a seedbed for rebirth, but also to be a tool of resurrection—guiding us gently in the ways of restoration and wholeness, and into some version of new life.
>
> **—Rev. Grier Booker Richards**, PC (USA) pastor, Raleigh, North Carolina, author of *The Language of the Soul Conversation Guide and Journal*

Reading in Seasons of Grief and Loss

15 Recommended Books

Below is a list of 15 books exploring themes of grief and loss in deeply personal, poignant, and yet hopeful ways.

- *When the World Breaks Your Heart*, by Gregory Clapper
- *A Grace Disguised*, by Jerry Sittser
- *A Grief Observed*, by C. S. Lewis
- *A Long Letting Go*, by Marilyn McEntyre
- *The Deepest Place: Suffering and the Formation of Hope*, by Curt Thompson, M.D.
- *Where is God When It Hurts?*, by Philip Yancey
- *Our Greatest Gift*, by Henri J. M. Nouwen
- *Dessert First: Preparing for Death While Savoring Life*, by J. Dana Trent
- *Three Dog Life*, by Abigail Thomas
- *Everything Happens for a Reason (And Other Lies I've Loved)*, by Kate Bowler
- *An Incurable Faith*, by Andrea Herzer
- *Undone: A Modern Rendering of John Donne's Devotions*, edited by Philip Yancey
- *Grieving a Suicide*, by Albert Y. Hsu
- *Good Grief: A Companion for Every Loss*, by Granger E. Westberg
- *Beyond the Darkness: A Gentle Guide for Living with Grief and Thriving After Loss*, by Clarissa Moll

"Doubt is the skeleton in the closet of faith, and I know no better way to treat a skeleton than to bring it into the open and expose it for what it is: not something to hide or fear, but a hard structure on which living tissue may grow."

—Philip Yancey, *Reaching for the Invisible God*[1]

Chapter Ten
Reading in Seasons of Doubt and Fear

As an elementary school child, Shelly Satran lived in an unusual environment. Her dad was the warden of a North Dakota state prison, and the family's housing quarters backed onto that facility. It was an everyday experience for her to look out the window and see razor wire surrounding the prison property, and Shelly remembers thinking nothing of it.

It was just "home" for her.

But the odd positioning of the light switches in her old house and the darkness that pervaded it until they were turned on—now, that was another thing. Like many structures of its era, the light switches of the Satran family's government-issued house were positioned not right next to the doors as you entered but rather, were on far walls, requiring adults and children alike to walk across a darkened room in order to depress the switch and illuminate the house.

Reflecting back on those years, Satran remembers one distinct evening—probably in fifth or sixth grade, "old enough to be home alone, even next to a prison," she says—when her school friend's mother brought her home at night. Her parents were not yet home, and the house was utterly dark. The prison's razor wire may have glistened in the North Dakota moonlight, but even if it did no light brightened the house.

Sensing, perhaps, Shelly's reluctance to go into the unlit home, the mother's friend said, "How about I go in ahead of you and help turn on the lights?"

The friend's mother walked ahead of Shelly, entered the house and flipped on the old switches to brighten the home and create a sense of safety, a sense of coming out of the dark. Her fear evaporated in the presence of the light.

"I felt like she was an angel in that moment, knowing what I needed without my saying anything or having to be embarrassed about it," Satran recalled.[2]

Angels of Light in the Darkness

I have never lived near a prison, but I have traveled through seasons of fear and doubt and, like Shelly, needed an "angel" to walk just ahead or alongside me to be a light in the darkness. At times, it has been my wife or a friend, mentor, or counselor who offered companionship and guidance. At other times I have found the illumination I've needed through reading the words of others who have gone before me wrestling with similar fears, dealing with similar doubts. In some cases, their words offered companionship by flipping switches and illuminating darkness. At other times, it came through their reminders to stay with the questions, to dwell in the shadows of the moon just a bit to see what I might learn there, how I might grow, how my faith might be strengthened.

Although I didn't begin to attend church regularly until I was in my late teens, the church that I came into at that time often seemed unwelcoming of acknowledgments of fear and particularly of doubt, even if it was largely unspoken. Hymns and praise songs heralded certainty. They exhorted us to trust and obey, to never have a doubt or fear because we always knew that God is near. I distinctly recall one conversation with a church leader who said that there is a danger for someone who read as widely as he suspected I did, because doing so would lead to questions that could only negatively impact my faith, not build it up.

Reflecting back on those early days getting rooted in the church and the Christian faith, I can see the ways in which I took on that cloak myself, perhaps without knowing it. I searched for and embraced certainty over mystery; pursued fearlessness over acknowledging the places where fear reigned and needed to be carefully tended.

But ultimately, it did not work. I could not continue to wear that cloak.

The Wisdom of Alex Adamson

In 1986, a just-released, maroon-covered hardcover with an arresting title arrived in my bookstore from a Texas-based publisher: *The Myth of Certainty.* A quote attributed to Blaise Pascal, author of *Pensées*, also adorned the cover, suggesting that "we must know where to doubt, where to feel certain, and where to submit." The author was Daniel Taylor, then an associate professor of English at Bethel College in Minnesota, and the book was primarily a treatise on the challenges and joys of being what he called a "reflective Christian."

I was drawn in by the combination of the book's title and Pascal's admonition. I read it within days of its arrival, and *The Myth of Certainty* became a touchstone book nearly forty years ago and remains so today.

Taylor said that being a reflective person is not to be confused with amassing information nor with intelligence. Instead, that person is "a question asker—one who finds in every experience and assertion something that requires further investigation. He or she is a stone-turner, attracted to the creepy-crawly things that live under rocks, and behind human pronouncements." To be reflective, he said, is "to be sensitive to and fascinated by the complexity of things."[3]

As I read *The Myth of Certainty,* I sensed a kindred spirit in the author, and also in a fictional character whose story Taylor threaded throughout the book. He called the fictional portions the "adventures and misadventures of one particular reflective Christian by the name of Alex Adamson."[4]

Years later in correspondence, Taylor told me that he had a two-fold prompt for writing *The Myth of Certainty.*

The first was "a years-long series of conversations in my office with students who were in a tug of war with their better angels regarding faith and all the questions that faith raises for a certain kind of mind," Taylor said. "And, as the writing went on, a realization that I was writing to explain to myself my own life. I had just led a group of students for a semester-long study abroad program in Europe in 1983, during which some of these issues arose again. I had a sabbatical due on return and decided to write a book about these things. And that turned out to be *The Myth of Certainty.* Writing it was intended to help others, but had the added benefit of helping me understand myself and my own faith journey."[5]

Reading Taylor's philosophically tinged prose and his book's fictional vignettes of Alex's misadventures, I came away believing that while being a question-asker in the church may not be *easy*, it was not incompatible with being *faithful.* He was one of the authors who flipped a switch, illuminating the dark that descended from time to time as I turned over rocks and saw creepy-crawly things that lived there. Taylor's own discipline of reading is what made him able to write with impact on the lives of others.

"In writing the book, I was not passing on my own wisdom; I was processing the wisdom available from the work of others as it flowed through my own life, people like Pascal and Kierkegaard, and trying to share that wisdom with others," Taylor told me. "Had I not been a reader, I would today be less a Christian, and much less able to be helpful to others."

Dealing with Our Doubts

Alister McGrath, a professor of science and religion at Oxford University, has been another helpful guide in thinking about doubt. In his book *Doubting: Growing Through the Uncertainties of Faith*, McGrath suggests that faith and doubt are not mutually exclusive, as some tacitly or directly suggest, but faith and *unbelief* are.

"Doubt often means asking questions or voicing uncertainties from the standpoint of faith. You believe—but you have difficulties with that faith, or are worried about it in some way," he writes. "Doubt is probably a permanent feature of the Christian life. It's like some kind of spiritual growing pain. Sometimes it recedes into the background; at other times it comes to the forefront, making its presence felt with a vengeance."[6]

McGrath's book takes seriously the doubts many of us have about a variety of topics including atheism, God, Scripture, Christ, the Resurrection—and also, doubts about ourselves. He emphasizes the primacy of discipleship of the mind in the midst of our questions and doubts. And reading is one of the key building blocks of that discipleship.

Philip Yancey, who grew up in the American South in a church tradition even more inhospitable to doubts and questions than mine, has said it's hard to read biographies of great people of faith—church reformer Martin Luther, Puritan Richard Baxter, evangelist Dwight L. Moody, mystic and prolific writer Evelyn Underhill, and others—without encountering a "skeleton of doubt" upon which their great faith grew. And looking at the lives of Adam, Sarah, Jacob, Job, Jeremiah, Jonah, Thomas, Martha, and Peter in the Bible we, likewise, see a faithful follower of God "who questions, squirms, and rebels yet still remains loyal."[7]

Doubt and Fear

Through their writings, Taylor, McGrath, Yancey, and other authors have modeled for me what it means to acknowledge and live in the midst of questions, even of doubts. They make a strong case that it is better to put those "skeletons" out into the light rather than trying to hide them or being fearful of them.

In my more than 40-year journey as a follower of Christ, I have found that to be true. And contrary to that church leader many years ago, the act of reading—broadly, from contrasting viewpoints and diverse voices—has had the effect not of undermining faith, but of strengthening it and delivering a faith, in the famous words of Oliver Wendell Holmes, born out of "simplicity on the far side of complexity."[8]

Authors as Companions: Reading in Seasons of Doubt and Fear

> The pathway through doubt and fear is not so much muscularity or willpower or doctrinal certainty, but love. Fear is overwhelming when we face it alone, and so is doubt, but when we have companions to help us walk forward with wobbly knees, that's where hope is found even if uncertainty persists.
>
> I wonder who your companions are in these liminal moments. Some of mine have been Henri Nouwen, Frederick Buechner, Barbara Brown Taylor, and Mark Buchanan. When reading these authors, I have the sense of sitting in a room with them, or maybe an English pub, having long conversations about how complex and confusing life can be. Their words don't calm all my fears, nor do they resolve all my doubts, but they aren't intended to. The authors I appreciate most are writing to walk alongside us, and it is so good not to be alone on this journey of life.
>
> —**Mark R. McMinn**, co-author of *An Invitation to Slow*, author of *The Science of Virtue*

Reading in Seasons of Doubt and Fear

15 Recommended Books

Below you'll find a list of books that have been companions during seasons of fear and doubt. The authors approach the topics in unique and sometimes divergent ways, but all have been a source of instruction.

- *The Myth of Certainty*, by Daniel Taylor
- *How Not to Be Afraid*, by Gareth Higgins
- *Companions in the Darkness: Seven Saints Who Struggled with Depression and Doubt*, by Diana Gruver
- *Learning to Walk in the Dark*, by Barbara Brown Taylor
- *Reaching for the Invisible God*, by Philip Yancey
- *Wandering Toward God: Finding Faith amid Doubts and Big Questions*, by Travis Dickinson
- *Doubting: Growing Through the Uncertainties of Faith*, by Alister McGrath
- *Overcoming Anxiety, Worry and Fear*, by Gregory L. Jantz with Ann McMurray
- *I Have My Doubts: How God Can Use Your Uncertainty to Reawaken Your Faith*, by Philip Ryken
- *Ruthless Trust*, by Brennan Manning
- *Fear and Faith: Finding the Peace Your Heart Craves*, by Trillia Newbell
- *When Faith Fails: Finding God in the Shadow of Doubt*, by Dominic Done
- *Freedom from My Fears: 40 Meditations on David's Psalms and Prayers*, by Harold Myra
- *After Shock: Searching for Honest Faith When Your World Is Shaken*, by Kent Annan
- *Mere Christianity*, by C. S. Lewis

"How does inhabiting the Story of God in liturgical time actually shape our lives? Here is the simple answer: by remembering and anticipating."

—Bobby Gross, *Living the Christian Year*[1]

Chapter Eleven
READING IN THE SEASONS OF THE LITURGICAL YEAR

Although it has been more than 20 years now, I still remember my first *Tenebrae* service as if it were yesterday. I recall the impact of the gradual descent into utter darkness as candle after candle was extinguished. I can hear the disarming, frightening if brief noise—a sound something like a stack of heavy books being dropped on a concrete floor—and then deafening silence in the church as congregants walked out without saying a word.

It was not like anything I had ever experienced in a church before. My attention had never been so heightened.

Tenebrae is a Latin word meaning "shadows" or "darkness," and it is practiced by Roman Catholic, Lutheran, and some Orthodox and Reformed parishes throughout the West. In the service of *Tenebrae*, we remember Christ's betrayal, agony in Gethsemane, and arrest, as well as the apostle Peter's denial, Pilate's accusations, and ultimately the Savior's crucifixion, death, and burial. These scenes are all brought to life as Gospel passages from Matthew 26 and 27 are read, songs are sung, and light is muted with the snuffing out, one by one, of each of the seven candles.

For me, the descent of *Tenebrae* was an ascent—of attentiveness, of recognition, of experiential reminders of the work of Christ. And as one who had spent much of my adult life focused on the intellectual, logical, and apologetic aspects of the Christian faith, this ascent was a gift for which I remain deeply grateful today.

The Gifts of Change

One of the unexpected gifts of a move many years ago from a nondenominational, evangelical church context to one rooted in the sacraments and the liturgical calendar (or Christian year) was a whole new world of worship experiences it opened up, like the *Tenebrae* service. The shift also opened up a new world of reading through the seasons of the church year.

I'd long read devotional reflections for Christmas, of course, gathered with my family around a fire with hot chocolate in hand. Easter readings were less frequent in those days, though they occasionally happened. But the liturgical calendar was something altogether new—Advent, Christmas, Epiphany, Lent, Easter, Pentecost, and Ordinary Time. I discovered new opportunities for spiritual reflection as I began to journey through the church year both in congregational life and on my own, as I began to read prayer books and other works that served as companions through the church calendar. Occasionally a good friend and I would read the same book, like Henri Nouwen's *Show Me the Way*, as we recognized together the 40 days of Lent that begins with Ash Wednesday. Most of the time, I was simply reading on my own throughout the week, and with the congregation on Sunday.

As I have reflected on why this shift to "living the Christian year" has been so important to me, I've come to believe it is simply this: Each year, with the church around the world, I *enter into* the Christ story. I am *reminded* of its dramatic elements. I am *strengthened* to continue to follow the risen Christ in hope and love. I am, in the words of my friend Bobby Gross, "remembering and anticipating."

The late Walter Wangerin Jr., whom I introduced to you in the chapter on reading fiction, captures this idea more eloquently than I can when he says:

> Throughout my life it has been my good fortune to experience the story of Jesus with every turning of every year. The number of the years of my unfolding age is also the number of times I've traveled with my Lord from his birth to his death to his triumphant rising again. And because the story has been more than *told* to me; because it has *surrounded* me like a weather; because it *comprehends* me as a house does its inhabitants or a mother does her child, the life of Christ has shaped mine. My very being has been molded in him.[2]

Wangerin goes on to suggest that he thinks of the story of Christ as a five-act drama, with Act 1 being Advent, followed by Christmas, Epiphany, Lent, and finally Easter. He says that "these are the acts that have driven my whole person so dramatically close to Jesus."[3]

Stories of the Christian Year

The late Eugene Peterson, a contemporary and friend of Wangerin's when the two were a part of the literary gathering known as the Chrysostom Society, also has an interesting view of the Christian year. Peterson suggests that the year is rightly divided into two parts, what he calls the Lord's half-year and the Christian's half-year.

"Our Lord's half-year, from Advent to Ascension, tells the stories of our Lord's arrival, life, death, and resurrection," Peterson writes in his edited collection *Stories of the Christian Year*, made up of essays by his friends in the Chrysostom Society. "The Christian's half-year (from Pentecost to Christ the King) tells the stories of our reception of his Spirit, our participation in the trinity, our long discipleship as a communion of saints, our death and resurrection under the overarching sovereignty of Christ."[4]

Stories.

That is the key for Peterson. And that is the key for living the Christian year—inhabiting the story of Christ, of Christ's provision for us, of God's promise to us, in and through Christ. Year after year.

An Early Signpost of the Ascent

In the mid-1980s as part of a bookselling convention in Washington, D.C., I attended a reception at the Kennedy Center for the Performing Arts. I remember that a host of musicians were there that night, but I don't recall who they were. I also remember it was something of a "black tie" affair, and that I felt out of place with the attire I had brought to that convention, nothing remotely formal about it. What I most remember, though, was that all of us in attendance were given a leather-like bound prayer book titled *Disciplines for the Inner Life*, edited by Bob Benson and his son, Michael W. Benson. With daily invocations, Psalms, Scripture readings, and selections for meditation arranged thematically but with hints of what I would come to know as the liturgical year, it was my introduction to this way of reading not merely to know or to answer questions about the faith that I may someday be asked but, rather, to cultivate deeply and spiritually inward graces of a centered life and outward fruits of the inner life.

"Down through Christian history various spiritual principles, rules, disciplines and practices have aided the believer in the quest for a deeper knowledge of God. There were liturgies, lectionaries, prayer books and guides for the hours and days of one's spiritual journey," Bob and Michael wrote. "One of the common threads of all of these tools of spirituality was the recognition of the need for constancy in the establishment and deepening of a person's spiritual relationship with God. And underlying the writings of all those whose works have stood the test of time is the theme of faithfulness and regularity in spiritual practice."[5]

I have kept that volume presented at the Kennedy Center in 1985 with me for 40 years, and it's among the most well-used books in my library. Its introduction to the lectionary and to readings on a range of topics from desire and silence to distractions and service laid the groundwork for a movement into observing and deeply experiencing the liturgical calendar in the years to come.

In her book *The Riches of Your Grace: Living in the Book of Common Prayer*, author and journalist Julie Lane-Gay captures well the essence of why the liturgical year has become sustaining for me.

> The twelve-month calendar is a formidable force. Thanksgiving, tax deadlines, the last day of our summer holidays—their specific dates come to mind far more quickly than the first day of Advent or the end of Lent. But increasingly it's the liturgical seasons that appeal to me more. They carry a joy, a deeper goodness, a colorfulness. In the midst of deadlines and horrid world news, I remind myself I am in Advent and God himself is calling to me in these dark days of early winter; there is more going on than what I feel. In Easter I try to find ways to seize joy, or as poet Wendell Berry says so brilliantly at the end of one of his poems, "Practice resurrection." Returning each year to the stories of His beckoning, His coming, His explaining, His giving Himself, His redeeming us, and at last, His staying with us, I remember these events are our story, they're the time we live in, they're God revealing Himself to each of us in the Lord Jesus.[6]

Reading Through the Church Year in Community

It was Pastor James Honig who watered the seeds planted by Bob Benson through *Disciplines for the Inner Life* when he warmly received me into a liturgical congregation many years later. Honig, who now pastors a church in Door County, Wisconsin, has long believed that thriving congregations are also learning congregations.

"As a community, we cultivate the discipline of learning together, of being open to new ideas, of being open to the places the Spirit is leading. Of course, we listen and learn together from the Scriptures, but there is much beyond the Bible that we can learn together," Honig told me recently, as we recalled studying a Lenten reader together as a congregation. "It has been a regular part of my leadership team meetings that we will be reading together; in that group, particularly about the dynamics of congregational life and vitality."[7]

Leading up to the Lenten season, Honig purchased several cases of Walter Wangerin's book *Reliving the Passion*, a book he had previously read and enjoyed on his own. He decided to use it as a congregational study during the next Lenten season.

"We already had the tradition of offering the congregation a Lenten devotional booklet. Those, however, were offered primarily as tools for individual devotion," Honig reminded me. "With the Wangerin book *Reliving the Passion,* we took that to another level and really dove into it as a community study. We used the reflections in daily morning prayer; some of the women's groups used it as their monthly study; and a few small groups formed just for the season to reflect on the book. So, beyond the broad goal of nurturing a learning congregation, the goal for this particular season was to create a sense of unity around common devotion and conversation for the season."

Wangerin drove some two hours from his home in Valparaiso, Indiana, to our congregation in Chicago's western suburbs to preach on Palm Sunday the year our congregation studied his book.

He was not in good health, but he came anyway. Honig said that Wangerin "was thrilled to be in a place that had broadly paid so much attention to his work, and the congregation was thrilled to have him with us to preach. It was really a day of mutual joy for both congregation and preacher, even though it was Passion Sunday and the tone was rather somber."

The Importance of the Liturgical Year

I have heard some who were raised in a church that placed a strong emphasis on liturgy and the church calendar say that they felt freed when they were no longer a part of a congregation that observed the liturgical year. It had seemed rote to them, uninspiring, like a relic from the past. Others have told me that they simply don't understand it all. It seems complicated, complex, too much to follow amid the business of modern-day life. Listening to the Spirit, all of us must find the sacred pathway to deep communion with God and sustenance in worship, and I understand that living the church year isn't for everyone. But for many of us, it is a life-giving discipline, and reading through the seasons of the church calendar gives us exposure to saints who have gone before us and saints who walk alongside us. Books like Leland Ryken's *40 Favorite Hymns for the Christian Year*, Sylvie Vanhoozer's lavishly illustrated *The Art of Living in Season: A Year of Reflections for Everyday Saints*, or Bobby Gross's *Living the Christian Year: Time to Inhabit the Story of God*, and many others shed light on a pilgrim's path as we journey through both the "Lord's half" and the "Christian's half" of each passing year.

Reading in the Seasons of the Liturgical Year

> I was nudged into the liturgical year. First the Book of Common Prayer, then a stunning Lenten reflection, then something pastor Eugene Peterson wrote, "I was convinced that it was critically important to pay more attention to what God does than what I do: to find daily, weekly, yearly rhythms that would get that awareness into my bones." Initially I pondered my problematic attention and "bones," but soon I realized I needed to change, to concentrate on the Prayer Book's Collects and colors, seasonal plants—and daily reading. The anthology *God With Us* in Advent, N. T. Wright in Lent, Fleming Rutledge in Epiphany are staples. In Ordinary Time I read stories of, well, ordinaries: *Hannah Coulter*, *So Young Brave and Handsome*, *Godric*—tales that tell

me who I am, that quietly shed light on who God is, who Christ is—and of all the ways He is holding time, loving into my bones, and hopefully out again.

—**Julie Lane-Gay**, author of *The Riches of Your Graces: Living in the Book of Common Prayer*

Reading in the Seasons of the Liturgical Year

15 Recommended Resources

What follows is a list of books that have been touchstones for celebrating and living into the liturgical (or Christian) year in community with others and on my own as a spiritual practice. The resources reflect a variety of Christian traditions and theological perspectives.

- *Living the Christian Year*, by Bobby Gross
- *Disciplines of the Inner Life*, by Bob Benson and Michael W. Benson
- *Small Surrenders: A Lenten Journey*, by Emilie Griffin
- *Season of Beauty: A Lent and Easter Treasury of Readings, Poems, and Prayers*, by the editors of Paraclete Press
- *One Great Love: An Advent and Christmas Treasury of Readings, Poems, and Prayers*, by the editors of Paraclete Press
- *O Come, O Come, Emmanuel*, by Jonathan Gibson (Advent to Epiphany)
- *O Sacred Head, Now Wounded*, by Jonathan Gibson (Pascha to Pentecost)
- *Sounding the Seasons: Poetry for the Christian Year*, by Malcom Guite
- *Reliving the Passion*, by Walter Wangerin Jr.

- *Stories for the Christian Year*, edited by Eugene H. Peterson
- *Where the Eye Alights: Phrases for the Forty Days of Lent*, by Marilyn McEntyre
- *The Divine Hours*, by Phyllis Tickle
- *The Art of Living in Season: A Year of Reflections for Everyday Saints*, by Sylvie Vanhoozer
- *The Liturgical Year: The Spiraling Adventure of the Spiritual Life*, by Joan Chittister
- *The Riches of Your Grace: Living in the Book of Common Prayer*, by Julie Lane-Gay

"The easiest door to open for a child, usually, is one that leads to something you love yourself. All good teachers know this. And all good teachers know the ultimate reward: the marvelous moment when the spark you are breathing on bursts into a flame that henceforth will burn brightly on its own."

—Arthur Gordon, *A Touch of Wonder*[1]

Chapter Twelve
Reading in Seasons of Wonder and Discovery

Savannah, Georgia, is a picturesque, history-laden southern American city with Gothic churches lining its cobblestone streets. Signature Spanish moss drapes from live oak trees in the city's parks and squares. Trolleys and horse-drawn carriages ferry visitors through the historic district, passing Victorian homes and antebellum mansions in what was once the capital of the state. From Bay Street one can see the Savannah River carrying barges and ships to and from the Atlantic coast 18 miles to the east.

Those coastal waters are where a young Arthur Gordon saw the stars fall and his young life was first marked with wonder.

Gordon was a former *Guideposts* editor and the author of 14 books including the 1974 bestseller *A Touch of Wonder*, a collection of essays and short stories. He was also a member of one of Savannah's most prominent families. His aunt Juliette Gordon Low founded the Girl Scouts of America in 1912, and its first chapter was launched in Savannah. Arthur's great-grandfather William Washington Gordon was an American politician and the founder of the Central of Georgia

Railroad (now a part of Norfolk Southern Railway). A towering monument in the city's Wright Square pays tribute to him.[2]

But it was Arthur's father whom I wish I'd met. From the pages of his son's book, he seems like a remarkable man—and like someone I aspire to be.

The Night the Stars Fell

"One summer night in a seaside cottage, a small boy felt himself lifted from bed. Dazed with sleep, he heard his mother murmur about the lateness of the hour, heard his father laugh. Then he was borne in his father's arms, with the swiftness of a dream, down the porch steps, out onto the beach," Gordon writes in "The Night the Stars Fell."[3]

Despite the late hour and the awareness of a young boy's need for sleep, young Arthur's father knew a spectacular show was waiting, and there was wonder to be found. Undeterred, off they went into the blackness of the night.

After they came to their seaside destination, Arthur looked into the overhead sky ablaze with stars. "Watch!," Arthur's father exclaimed, "and incredibly, as he spoke, one of the stars moved. In a streak of golden fire, it flashed across the astonished heavens. And before the wonder of this could fade, another star leaped from its place, and then another, plunging toward the restless sea. 'What is it?' the child whispered. 'Shooting stars,' his father said. 'They come every year on certain nights in August. I thought you'd like to see the show.'"[4]

That image of father and son, of stars falling from the sky, of bright encounters in the world of wonder they inhabited off the coast of Savannah in the 1920s, captivated me from the first time I read the book. I longed to be that kind of father (or grandfather), to eschew things like bedtimes and family rhythms and "sane decisions" in favor of stars and constellations, in favor of stories and wonder.

I return to the pages of *A Touch of Wonder* every year, rereading and being drawn in as if for the first time. Revisiting its pages and being filled with wonder once again and prompted to try my level best to never let the curiosity of childhood evaporate amid jobs and tasks and expectations and the aging process. It is my prayer for myself (and for you) that wonder and discovery are not simply a season but a hallmark of our entire lives from our first utterance of "why" as a small child until we take our last breath—and all the seasons in between.

Marriage, a Book, and a Life of Wonder

When Cindy and I were first married, we received a $3.95 paperback book as a gift from a wise, older man named Ward. He was a seminary professor who was well-versed in Greek and Hebrew, but his gift was a copy of Arthur Gordon's unpretentious book of stories *A Touch of Wonder*.

"This book has meant as much to me as any other," our friend said. "Read it and celebrate the gift of bright encounters together." In essence, Ward was, in our first year of marriage, asking us to cultivate an appreciation of the wonder of life, of living, of one another. And he chose a book to foster that.

A Touch of Wonder is full of simple things, really. Stories of Gordon's children. Tales of days spent fishing on the Savannah River. A story of a magical staircase in the American Southwest. A poignant essay illustrating the ways in which fear often holds us back from changes we need to make. In the introduction, Gordon writes about the underlying theme:

"Almost always there's a lot more to these commonplace happenings than meets the casual eye—and most people would find a lot more in them if only they would pause and look and feel and care just a bit more than they do."[5]

Now, more than four decades after receiving that gift from our friend, we both recall Gordon's words and marvel at the truth they contain. It's through our marriage that we've each encountered windows to the world that, without the other person, might have been shuttered from view. And despite what we expected, our most cherished moments aren't just the biggest ones—such as our wedding or the days we brought children into the world or the day one of us landed the job we'd always longed for. Instead, we've found that the simple events, the daily encounters, have offered the richest experiences.

Before we met, for instance, my idea of classical music was the Moody Blues' 1967 hit "Nights in White Satin." But when we became friends, and shared our music collections with each other, we listened to one of Cindy's favorite musical pieces, Rachmaninoff's "Piano Concerto No. 2." Through that single window a vista to the wonders of classical music was opened for me: Mahler, Gershwin, Vivaldi, Bach, and much more. Cindy's musical tastes also ran the gamut, but until our journey together began, they didn't include the spiritually flavored folk-rock vistas of Van Morrison, Bruce Cockburn, or Brooks Williams. Since I introduced her to them, these musicians have become an integral part of her life.

Traveling has afforded us other windows through which to peer. Cindy has a passion for enjoying the natural world—the star fields of a desert sky, the awkwardly shaped cacti in Joshua Tree National Park, a red-tailed hawk spiraling upward on a thermal. On one occasion, we carved out an afternoon to go hiking in Michigan along a dune-drifted shoreline. Another time, we opted to journey to the town where I grew up. We trekked back to the vacant lots where I played baseball, visited old schools, and picked our way along the railroad trestle I walked daily as a kid. I shared memories that helped Cindy make more sense of my "story." These times spent together forged deeper bonds between us, helping us learn a little more about what makes us who we are.

And then there are books.

We're both passionate readers, though she has me beat, on average, with ten books read for every one that I've finished. Indeed, the librarians who staff our local public library tease me about how tall her stack of check-outs is compared to mine each time we pull up to the drive-up window to retrieve titles we've put on reserve. Our book stacks reflect wildly different genres and topics. Yet the commitment to share our individual literary encounters—reading passages aloud to each other before we go to sleep or travel in the car, sharing the excitement of a new author or a new idea—has marked our lives in significant ways. I shared my copy of Annie Dillard's *Pilgrim at Tinker Creek* with her, and it became her favorite book. She, in turn, introduced me to the world of fiction—a genre I used to dismiss for the most part—and its power to captivate, teach, and entertain.

Throughout the pages of *World of Wonders* I have put forth the suggestion that books are a way that our lives can be opened up, expanded, sharpened, deepened, and made more vibrant and whole. Reading as part of our practice of spiritual disciplines is one way that we can cultivate faithfulness and lives marked by wonder and by the fruit of the spirit. And if there is a single book that forms the foundation for that belief it is Gordon's 1974 masterpiece. The original edition's subtitle was *A Book to Help People Stay in Love With Life*, though I have always believed a more apt description would be "a book to help people maintain curiosity all their days."

"I think that all too often our world seems so un-miraculous because it seems so familiar," the novelist Steven James writes in his foreword to a later edition of Gordon's book, simply titled *Wonder*. "Habit and routine dull our senses to the glory of the universe, to the marvel of the moments unfolding all around us. The greatest philosophers, poets and prophets have always known this and tried to wake us up to the glory, to the wonder."[6]

Seasons of Wonder and Discovery

The late Lewis B. Smedes was a writer whose books repeatedly called his readers to maintain a sense of wonder in the midst of all the wounds and challenges and sadness of the world we inhabit.

"It takes grace in our time to keep our minds open to wonder, to be ready for the tug from God, the push from the Spirit, and the revelation of deep things from the hearts of ordinary people," Smedes wrote. "It takes grace, but it is a great gift. If you have a place in your life where your eyes can still gape, your knees quiver, and your mind boggle, you are open for wonder. And, open to wonder, you are ready for God's surprises, even the greatest of all; that it can be all right when everything is wrong."[7]

Many of us, perhaps, think of seasons of wonder and discovery as being more for the young. Smedes didn't buy that, and neither do I. Curiosity, wonder, and discovery can and should be for all of us. Yes, the world we live in is full of brokenness. Wars and rumors of wars are with us at all times. Disease, famine, and the devastating results of climate change are with us each day. Is pondering the notion of wonder wise in such a world?

Karen Wright Marsh is a writer who believes the answer is a resounding *yes!* In her book *Wake Up to Wonder*, Marsh acknowledges that we live in a fragile, unsettled time and that talk about wonder might make some just a bit uncomfortable or seem to be a leisure we simply don't have time for. *Don't we know what's going on all around us? Don't we know all of the wrongs we need to right?* And yet she extends invitations to wonder through vivid sketches of the lives of 22 people from around the world, some well-known—Martin Luther, Augustine, Howard Thurman, and Dorothy Day—and others we may encounter for just the first time, such as Mabel Ping-Hua Lee, Ephrem the Syrian, Pandita Ramabai, and Lilias Trotter. At the conclusion of each portrait, we are invited into practices that foster wonder and amazement.

Wake Up to Wonder is doing for today's generation what *A Touch of Wonder* did for me four decades ago, and continues to do.

Whether reading *A Touch of Wonder*, *Wake Up to Wonder*, a children's classic such as Frances Hodgson Burnett's *The Secret Garden*, Antoine de Saint-Exupéry's *The Little Prince*—a timeless book for all ages, or innumerable other works well-known or not, developing and sustaining a life of curiosity, wonder, and discovery is not only important but is also possible. And as we do so, we model a life of wonder for those who will come behind us; we set light upon their paths.

A Light Remains

In the epilogue of the original paperback edition of *A Touch of Wonder,* readers encounter these words:

> There is not enough darkness in all the world to put out the light of one small candle...
>
> This inscription was found on a small, new gravestone after a devastating air raid on Britain in World War II. Some thought it must be a famous quotation, but it wasn't. The words were written by a lonely old lady whose pet had been killed by a Nazi bomb.
>
> I have always remembered those words, not so much for their poetry and imagery as for the truth they contain. In moments of discouragement, defeat or even despair, there are always certain things to cling to. Little things, usually: remembered laughter, the face of a sleeping child, a tree in the wind—in fact, any reminder of something deeply felt or dearly loved.
>
> No man is so poor as not to have many of these small candles. When they are lighted, darkness goes away . . . and a touch of wonder remains.[8]

For the curious and committed, books are a portal to these touches of wonder. They are those candles whose light overcomes darkness.

On Reading in Seasons of Wonder and Discovery

In a world as broken as it is breathtaking, sometimes we're gifted with a sudden thrill, a glimpse of God's power and goodness. A sunset stops us in our tracks. A long-held dream comes to fruition. A selfless act turns a day—or a life—around. And we feel . . . wonder.

Dwelling in words of wonder can defy the tendency to gloss over these "everyday" miracles, to harness them into touchstones of hope, assurance, comfort, and courage. In Job, God speaks of the wonders of His creation for four entire chapters—and in response, a man who had been utterly bereft says, "I know that you can do all things, and that no purpose of yours can be thwarted." (Job 42:1)

—**Amanda Dykes**, author of *A Pocketful of Wonder* and *Born of Gilded Mountains*

Reading in Seasons of Wonder and Discovery

15 Recommended Books

Below are 15 books to probe the themes of wonder, discovery, and curiosity that are a part of this chapter. But let this list simply be a start. There are so many others to discover!

- *A Touch of Wonder*, by Arthur Gordon (also published as *Wonder*)
- *Return to Wonder*, by Arthur Gordon
- *Wake Up to Wonder*, by Karen Wright Marsh
- *A Pocketful of Wonder: 50 Hands-On Adventures for Kids to Discover God's Creation*, by Amanda Dykes
- *The Secret Garden*, by Frances Hodgson Burnett
- *The Little Prince*, by Antoine de Saint-Exupéry
- *Walking in Wonder*, by John O'Donohue
- *When You Wonder, You're Learning*, by Greg Behr and Ryan Rydzewski

- *Adorning the Dark*, by Andrew Peterson
- *Recapturing the Wonder*, by Mike Cosper
- *Simple Wonders*, by Christopher de Vinck
- *Becoming Curious: A Spiritual Practice of Asking Questions*, by Casey Tygrett
- *The Power of Wonder*, by Monica C. Parker
- *An Invitation to Slow*, by Mark R. McMinn and Lisa Graham McMinn
- *One Long River of Song: Notes on Wonder*, by Bryan Doyle

"Reading makes possible the connection between our minds and the near magical notions drawn up from our impossible hearts."

—Christopher de Vinck, *The Wall Street Journal*, 1993[1]

Conclusion
NURTURING A LIFE OF READING

There is a word that is off limits in my wife's and my home and with all members of our family, especially our grandchildren. All six of them know they can never utter it or succumb to the temptation to even *hint* at it.

It's the "B" word.

In a world awash with books to read, wonders to discover, places to metaphorically (or literally) visit, ideas to explore, people to meet, and character to cultivate, we should never be *bored*. How could we be?

And so the word is off limits in our family.

But as they have gotten older, I've observed that none of the six even need to be reminded not to use the word. Their lives are filled with curiosity. A mixture of physical, intellectual, relational, and spiritual pursuits marks their lives—each of them, in unique ways. And as I step back and watch I marvel at their growth, the ways in which they wake up each day to wonder. For all six, reading is among the core practices that fill their days, and gift ideas for birthdays and holidays often include books they are anxious to read.

In research that undergirded their book *Reading in the Wild*, an exploration of keys to cultivating lifelong reading habits, authors

Donalyn Miller and Susan Kelley identified five habits or characteristics of young readers who become the type of reader that I earnestly want to be throughout my remaining years and see my grandchildren be as they grow up. The kind of reader I hope *you* are, or may become, or will continue to be.

Miller and Kelley call these people "wild readers," but other words we could assign include avid, lifelong, voracious. While their research was rooted in younger readers, I believe their five descriptors are applicable to all of us:[2]

1. Regardless of the pace or demands of their lives, wild readers dedicate time to read.

2. They are confident in self-selecting reading materials, rather than engaging only with works that are assigned or recommended by others in positions of authority or influence.

3. They enjoy talking about books almost as much as reading them, and are sharing books and the ideas they encountered in them with others.

4. These readers have plans well beyond what they are currently reading, anticipating new topics to dig into, new authors and genres to look at, or the next volume in a series of impact.

5. Wild readers often show strong preferences for genres, authors, and topics they desire to read and carry that with them over time.

Do those characteristics look familiar to you and to your reading life? If not, might they become markers in the years ahead?

There is a world of wonders waiting to be opened through the pages of Scripture and other books, works that guide us and serve as companions throughout the seasons of our life. And like the musician who pushes himself to expand his repertoire, or the athlete who drives herself to achieve greater results individually or collectively as a team, we are served well to stretch ourselves and our reading beyond what is comfortable, beyond what is known, beyond what is easy as we practice reading as a spiritual discipline.

"A book that requires nothing from you might offer the same diversion as that of a television sitcom, but it is unlikely to provide intellectual, aesthetic, or spiritual rewards long after the cover is closed," Karen Swallow Prior writes in *On Reading Well*. "Therefore, even as you seek books that you will enjoy reading, demand ones that make demands on you: books with sentences so exquisitely crafted that they must be reread, familiar words used in fresh ways, new words so evocative that you are compelled to look them up, and images and ideas so arresting that they return to you unbidden for days to come."[3]

May this be true of us all as we become "wild readers" and open doors through the wide, wide, wonderful world of reading.

A Note About the Book Lists

Each of the chapters in *World of Wonders* concludes with a list of a dozen or more books either referenced in the material or which reinforce the content I've shared or serve as a way to go deeper. In some cases they reflect some of my favorite books in a given genre or topical realm. I have made an effort to draw from a diverse set of authors, theological perspectives, or literary approaches in building those lists.

In his book *Take and Read—Spiritual Reading: An Annotated List*, the late Eugene Peterson chose to include in his lists only books by authors who were no longer living and whose work had stood the test of time, whether decades or centuries. In building my list of recommended books included at the end of each chapter, I have chosen a different path. You will find a mixture of books both contemporary and classic, and in doing so I recognize that some of the works may or may not still be read decades from now. But they do, I believe, have a potency for us today.

In the lists in this book, you will find only the title and author. However, at the website JeffreyCrosby.net, I have posted an annotated listing, chapter-by-chapter, briefly covering why the books were chosen, who published them, and what you can expect if you read them.

I encourage you to use these lists as a place to explore more deeply and widely the subject matter in *World of Wonders.*

—Jeff Crosby

ACKNOWLEDGEMENTS

I am indebted to many booksellers whose work has helped form me into the reader that I am today, but I extend my special thanks to three who have had the most formative impact: Byron and Beth Borger at Hearts & Minds Books in Dallastown, Pennsylvania; Rick and Susan Lewis at Logos Bookstore in Dallas, Texas; and Warren Farha and the staff of Eighth Day Books in Wichita, Kansas. Your work represents a bright, shining light in the world. I am grateful, as well, for The Bookstore in Glen Ellyn, Illinois, for serving our local community with excellence and a wonderful assortment of books.

I'm grateful to the team at Paraclete Press, whose books I have long admired and been nurtured by. In particular, thanks go to Lillian Miao and Robert Edmonson for your support of this project and to Lexa Hale, Jenny Lynch, and Danielle Bushnell, whose marketing and publicity work will help the book reach readers in the days to come. A special thanks to former Paraclete Press marketing and publicity manager Rachel McKendree for early encouragement of this book, and to Tom Dean of Drop of Link Literary.

Thanks, as well, to Kaitlin Murphy for her editorial skills in helping to fine tune the manuscript. Her suggestions significantly improved the book.

Additionally, I offer my sincere appreciation to the published authors who shared with me their brief reflections at the conclusion of each chapter to amplify in their own artful ways the content I was attempting to convey: J. Brent Bill, Greg Bowman, Gregory Clapper, Amanda Dykes, Bob Fryling, Ed Gilbreath, J. K. Jones, Julie Lane-Gay, Mark McMinn, Ben Patterson, Grier Booker Richards, and Luci Shaw. I am grateful to Carolyn Weber for the gift of her foreword, setting up what follows it in these pages, and to Helen Lee for her insights on the importance of reading diverse books.

My six grandchildren—Ellie, Jack, Anna, Peggy, Tony, and Emily—are collectively the apple of my eye. May you continue to find a world of wonders as you read on your own, and with your Nonna and me! *Hey! Let's go read* Castaway Cats*!*

Finally, I dedicate this book to my wife, Cindy. For more than four decades, you have helped me pay attention to the wonders in the natural world and on the printed page. I'm grateful for your shared love of reading, writing, and a life of wonder.

Appendix: Reading and Journal Keeping

I have come to believe that reading as a spiritual discipline is enhanced by adding another discipline or spiritual practice alongside it: journal keeping.

In addition to underlining books (on occasion) or writing in the margins (rarely), I keep a series of journals at hand at all times as I am reading, whether as I travel or when at home or work. The movement of pen on paper as I reflect on what I am digesting in books and journals helps me to reinforce what I am reading.

If you are so inclined, there are specific journals for keeping track of reading which a local bookstore could order for you or you can find at an online retailer. Among the titles you can consider are these:

- *For the Love of Books: A Reading Journal* (Paper Peony Press)
- *The Bookish Companion*, by Karla Nikole
- *The Book Lover's Journal* (Peter Pauper Press)
- *Reading Journal*, by Rene J. Smith
- *Book Journal*, by Noteably

I have chosen to simply use blank journals, not those that help me keep a record of what I've read. The practice and purpose of journaling as I read is to record my observations on—

- What did I notice from today's reading?
- What was I prompted to reflect on?
- What questions did I have?
- What did I notice?
- What is prompted in the reading (whether a work of fiction, a poem, or nonfiction)?

Adele Ahlberg Calhoun, in her *Spiritual Disciplines Handbook*, suggests that journaling as a spiritual discipline is designed to help us be "alert to (our) life through writing and reflecting on God's presence and activity in, around and through (us)." A journal is "a tool for reflecting on God's presence, guidance and nurture in daily comings and goings."[1]

If reading is a part of listening to our life, journal keeping as we read is a means to understanding what we hear, what we believe, what questions we harbor, and what hopes we carry with us. Excellent resources for journaling are these:

- *Journaling as a Spiritual Practice*, by Helen Cepero (IVP)
- *Spiritual Journaling*, by Richard Peace (NavPress)
- *Journal Keeping*, by Luann Budd (IVP)
- *God Was With Me All Along*, by Mary Lou Redding (Upper Room Publishing)

Permissions

Ted Kooser's poem "Estate Sale," from *Splitting an Order.* Copyright © 2014 by Ted Kooser. Reprinted with the permission of The Permissions Company, LLC, on behalf of Copper Canyon Press, www.coppercanyonpress.org.

I extend my gratitude to InterVarsity Press for the permission to use a portion of the foreword written for Calvin Miller's book *The Singer* in an amended, slightly abbreviated version in chapter two.

A portion of chapter 7 was previously published in a different form in *Books and Culture* (online) in the article "Surprised by Oxford: A Memoir for Pilgrims Like Us," December 2011. Used with permission of Christianity Today, International.

A portion of chapter 11 was previously published in a different form in *Today's Christian Woman* in the article "Celebrate the Simple," summer 2002. Used with permission of Christianity Today International.

"Poetry Workshop," from *Eye of the Beholder* by Luci Shaw. Copyright 2018 by Luci Shaw. Used by permission of Paraclete Press.

Notes

Epigraph

[1] William Willimon, *Reading with Deeper Eyes* (Upper Room Books, 1998), 14.

Foreword

[1] Harold Bloom, *How to Read and Why* (Simon and Schuster, 2000), 19.
[2] Leland Ryken, et al., *The Discerning Reader: Christian Perspectives on Literature and Theory* (Baker, 1975), 10.
[3] C. S. Lewis, *An Experiment in Criticism* (Cambridge University Press, 1961), 137.
[4] Arthur Gordon, *Wonder: Moments that Keep you Falling in Love with Life* (Revell, 1974, repr. 2006), 270.

Introduction

[1] Liz Hoare, *Twelve Great Spiritual Writers* (SPCK Publishing, 2020), 9.
[2] Lewis, *An Experiment in Criticism*, quoted in C. S. Lewis, *The Reading Life*, ed. David C. Downing and Michael Maudlin (HarperOne, 2019), 4.
[3] Nancy M. Malone, *Walking a Literary Labyrinth* (Riverhead Books, 2003), 1.
[4] Richard J. Foster, *Celebration of Discipline 20th Anniversary Edition* (HarperSanFrancisco, 1998), 7.
[5] Donald S. Whitney, *Spiritual Disciplines for the Christian Life* (NavPress, 2014), 4.
[6] Mark Talbot, "Good Reading: Is Digital Culture Reducing Our Ability to Think Deeply?," from *Didaktikos Journal*, April 2019, 29.
[7] Anne Lamott, *Bird by Bird* (Anchor Books, 1994), 15.

Chapter One: Why Read At All?

[1] Roxanne J. Coady and Joy Johannessen, editors, *The Book That Changed My Life* (Gotham Books/Penguin Group USA, 2006), 134.
[2] Harold Bloom, *What to Read and Why* (Scribner, 2000), 21.
[3] David Brooks, *How to Know a Person* (Random House, 2023), 72.
[4] Anne Bogel, *I'd Rather Be Reading* (Tyndale House, 2018), 52.
[5] Steve McCurry and Paul Theroux, *Steve McCurry: On Reading* (Phaidon Press, 2016), 3.
[6] Calvin Miller, *The Singer: 25th Anniversary Edition* (InterVarsity Press, 2001), back cover.
[7] Sven Birkerts, *The Gutenberg Elegies* (Faber & Faber, 1994), 38.

[8] Eugene Peterson, *Eat This Book: A Conversation in the Art of Spiritual Reading* (Eerdmans, 2006), 11.

[9] Interview with J. K. Jones, June 2023.

Chapter Two: Reading as a Spiritual Discipline

[1] Byron Borger in *A Book for Hearts & Minds* (Square Halo Books, 2017), 16.

[2] Borger, *A Book for Hearts & Minds*, 15.

[3] Mark 12:30, ESV.

[4] Luke 10:27, ESV.

[5] Richard Foster, Dallas Willard, Phyllis Tickle, and Richard Rohr, *25 Books Every Christian Should Read* (HarperOne, 2011), ix.

[6] Craig Stoll, text of unpublished remarks delivered in Limuru, Kenya, February 20, 2023.

Chapter Three: Reading Scripture as a Spiritual Discipline

[1] Frederick Buechner, *Wishful Thinking* (Harper & Row, 1973), 9.

[2] Alex Goodwin, *The Bible Reset* (NavPress, 2023), 5.

[3] Andy Rau, "Where Do Verse and Chapter Numbers in the Bible Come From?," Bible Gateway, December 20, 2016.

[4] Goodwin, *The Bible Reset*, 5.

[5] Matthew Barrett, *Scripture as Divine Revelation*, TGC (The Gospel Coalition), www.thegospelcoalition.org/essay/scripture-divine-revelation/, accessed April 23, 2025.

[6] Barrett, *Scripture as Divine Revelation*.

[7] Buechner, *Wishful Thinking*, 10.

[8] Institute for Bible Reading: *Our Story*, https://instituteforbiblereading.org/our-story/, accessed April 23, 2025.

[9] Luann Budd, *Journal Keeping* (InterVarsity Press, 2002), 136.

[10] Budd, *Journal Keeping*, 136.

[11] Goodwin, *The Bible Reset*, 10.

Chapter Four: The Power of Story—Reading Fiction

[1] Eugene Peterson from *Reality and the Vision*, ed. Philip Yancey (Word Publishing, 1990), 26.

[2] Christine Seifert, "The Case for Reading Fiction," *Harvard Business Review*, March 6, 2020.

[3] Malcom Muggeridge, "Dostoyevsky Stricken," from *Plough* online, November 9, 2021.

[4] Yancey, *Reality and the Vision*, x.

[5] Yancey, *Reality and the Vision*, xi.

[6] Yancey, *Reality and the Vision*, x.

[7] Eugene Peterson, *Take and Read: An Annotated List of Spiritual Reading* (Eerdmans, 1996), 48–49.

[8] "Kent Haruf, 71, Acclaimed Novelist of Small-Town Life," William Yardley, *New York Times*, December 2, 2014.
[9] Yancey, *Reality and the Vision*, 5.

Chapter Five: The Power of Paying Attention—Reading Poetry

[1] Ted Kooser, *The Poetry Home Repair Manual* (Bison Books/University of Nebraska Press, 2005), 111.
[2] Laurence Perrine and Thomas R. Arp, *Sound and Sense: An Introduction to Poetry* (Harcourt, Brace Jovanovich, 1992), 3.
[3] Ted Kooser, "Estate Sale," from *Splitting An Order* (Copper Canyon Press, 2014), 29–36. Used with permission.
[4] Kathryn Lindskoog, *Creative Writing: For People Who Can't Not Write* (Zondervan, 1989), 117.
[5] Lindskoog, *Creative Writing*, 118.
[6] Lindskoog, *Creative Writing*, 122.
[7] Jill Peláez Baumgaertner, *Taking Root in the Heart* (Paraclete Press, 2023), xxii–xxiii.
[8] Marilyn McEntyre, *When Poets Pray* (Eerdmans, 2019), 2.
[9] "Why Does God Keep Making Poets," Tish Harrison Warren, *New York Times*, July 16, 2023.
[10] Luci Shaw, in a conversation with the author, September 2023.
[11] Luci Shaw, "Poetry Workshop," from *Eye of the Beholder* (Paraclete Press, 2018), 24.

Chapter Six: The Power of Perspective—Reading Diverse Voices

[1] Brandy Colbert, *Black Birds in the Sky* (Balzer + Bray/HarperCollins, 2021), 202.
[2] Personal message from Helen Lee to the author.
[3] Brandy Colbert, *Black Birds in the Sky*, 203.

Chapter Seven: The Power of Reflection—Reading Memoir

[1] Carolyn Weber, *Surprised by Oxford* (Thomas Nelson, 2011), 258–59.
[2] Nagham Mashraqi, "Memoir: An Underrated Genre," from *The Kudzu Review*, kudzureviewfsu.com, March 26, 2024.
[3] Carolyn Weber, *Surprised by Oxford* (Thomas Nelson, 2011), 2–3.
[4] Weber, *Surprised by Oxford*, 3.
[5] Weber, *Surprised by Oxford*, 3.
[6] Weber, *Surprised by Oxford*, 269.
[7] Weber, *Surprised by Oxford*, 409.
[8] Weber, *Surprised by Oxford*, 409.
[9] Diana Raab, PhD, "Why Is Memoir Writing Transformative?", *Psychology Today*, January 20, 2020.

[10] J. Dana Trent, *Between Two Trailers* (Convergent Books, 2024), xiii.
[11] Frederick Buechner, *Now and Then* (HarperSanFrancisco, 1983), 87, 92.

Chapter Eight: Reading in the Seasons of Family Life

[1] C. S. Lewis, *An Experiment in Criticism* (Cambridge University Press, 1961), 138.
[2] Terry Glaspey, *Book Lover's Guide to Great Reading* (InterVarsity Press, 2001), 177.
[3] William Kilpatrick, Gregory Wolfe, and Suzanne Wolfe, *Books that Build Character* (Simon & Schuster, 1994), 45.

Chapter Nine: Reading in Seasons of Grief and Loss

[1] Jerry Sittser, *A Grace Disguised* (Zondervan, 2004), 31.
[2] Laurence Gonzales, *Flight 232* (W.W. Norton, 2014), 1–2.
[3] C. S. Lewis, *A Grief Observed* (HarperOne, 1989), 17–18.
[4] Lewis, *A Grief Observed*, 10.
[5] Carrie Newcomer, in a post to Grateful.org.
[6] Gregory S. Clapper, *When the World Breaks Your Heart* (Upper Room Books, 1999), 106–107.

Chapter Ten: Reading in Seasons of Fear and Doubt

[1] Philip Yancey, *Reaching for the Invisible God* (Zondervan, 2000), 41.
[2] Personal correspondence between the author and Shelly Satran, July 2024.
[3] Daniel Taylor, *The Myth of Certainty* (Word Books, 1986), 16.
[4] Taylor, *The Myth of Certainty*, 31.
[5] Daniel Taylor, correspondence with the author, June 2024.
[6] Alister McGrath, *Doubting: Growing Through the Uncertainties of Faith* (InterVarsity Press, 2006), 14.
[7] Yancey, *Reaching for the Invisible God*, 42.
[8] Parker J. Palmer, "Simplicity on the Other Side of Complexity," from *On Being*, https://onbeing.org/blog/simplicity-on-the-other-side-of-complexity/, accessed April 23, 2025.

Chapter Eleven: Reading in the Seasons of the Liturgical Year

[1] Bobby Gross, *Living the Christian Year* (InterVarsity Press, 2009), 30.
[2] Walter Wangerin Jr., *Preparing for Jesus* (Zondervan, 1999), 11.
[3] Wangerin Jr., *Preparing for Jesus*, 11.
[4] Eugene Peterson, ed., *Stories of the Christian Year* (Macmillan, 1992), viii.
[5] Bob Benson and Michael W. Benson, *Disciplines for the Inner Life* (Word, 1985), xi.
[6] Julie Lane-Gay, *The Riches of Your Graces* (InterVarsity Press, 2024), 65.
[7] Author conversation with James Honig, April 2023.

Chapter Twelve: Reading in Seasons of Wonder and Discovery

[1] Arthur Gordon, *A Touch of Wonder* (Revell Publishing, 1974), 169.

[2] https://accesswdun.com/article/2002/1/200586 , accessed April 23, 2025.

[3] Gordon, *A Touch of Wonder*, 167.

[4] Gordon, *A Touch of Wonder*, 167.

[5] Gordon, *A Touch of Wonder*, 11.

[6] Steven James, from the foreword to *Wonder: Moments that Keep You Falling in Love with Life* by Arthur Gordon (Revell, 2006), 12.

[7] Lewis B. Smedes, *How Can It Be All Right When Everything Is All Wrong?* (Harold Shaw Publishers, 1999), 86.

[8] Arthur Gordon, *A Touch of Wonder* (Jove Books, 1978), 224.

Conclusion

[1] Christopher de Vinck, "Why I Read to My Children" (*Wall Street Journal*, November 1993).

[2] Donalyn Miller and Susan Kelley, *Reading in the Wild* (Jossey-Bass, 2014), xxiii-xxiv.

[3] Karen Swallow Prior, *On Reading Well: Exploring the Good Life Through Great Books* (Brazos Press, 2018), 17.

Appendix

[1] Adele Ahlberg Calhoun, *Spiritual Disciplines Handbook* (InterVarsity Press, 2015), 65.

ABOUT PARACLETE PRESS

PARACLETE PRESS IS THE PUBLISHING ARM of the Cape Cod Benedictine community, the Community of Jesus. Presenting a full expression of Christian belief and practice, we reflect the ecumenical charism of the Community and its dedication to sacred music, the fine arts, and the written word.

SCAN TO READ MORE

Learn more about us at our website:
www.paracletepress.com
or phone us toll-free at 1.800.451.5006

You may also be interested in

The Arts and the Christian Imagination (Kilby)

The Ecumenism of Beauty (Verdon)